Praise for THE BIG GUY UPSTAIRS

"Over the last twenty years of being friends with Rob Strong, I can't begin to count the number of times I've heard him tell a riveting, hilarious, gut-wrenching story that opens up all kinds of new insight and wisdom and thought: 'I wish everybody could hear that . . .' And now, with his first book, you can."

—**Rob Bell**, author of *What We Talk About When We Talk About God* and *Love Wins*

"Genuine, raw and real, Rob Strong is virtually guaranteed to comfort the disturbed while disturbing the comfortable. But for those who truly want to meet and walk with God, this book could be invaluable."

—**Rev. Dr. Clive Calver**, Walnut Hill Community Church

"Rob's down-to-earth language and honesty invite you to pull up your most comfortable chair and discover how he walks with his Creator. Rob unpacks what it means to not only believe in the Big Guy upstairs, but how to develop a meaningful relationship with Him."

—**David Mitchell**, World Vision International

"In an era when the ways we convey our genuine faith have grown dangerously irrelevant, while an unmet hunger for authentic connection with God only intensifies, Rob Strong delivers a poignant, delightful, witty, and profound re-look at the timeless questions of God embedded in our souls. Finally we have a text that cuts through the excruciatingly cliché language that normally get eyes rolling, and unpretentiously engages believers and non-believers alike in gut-level conversations about God."

—**Ron Carucci**, bestselling author, *Rising to Power* and *Leadership Divided*

"Rob is a gifted storyteller, able to draw you into his experiences—the good, the bad and the ugly—while relating each to God's heart and His desire to connect with each one of us. If you only read one book about a faith journey this year, choose THE BIG GUY UPSTAIRS. It will have you laughing, crying, and yearning to get beyond the edge of your life to the core of your purpose."

—Bernie Prusaczyk, Jr., CEO, Atlantic VIC

"Rob's book—like Rob himself—is refreshing, insightful, and inspiring. Spiritual seekers inside and outside the church will be surprised to find The Big Guy isn't nearly as distant or mysterious as they might have imagined."

—Rev. Dr. Bryan Wilkerson, Grace Chapel

"Do you have questions about what God is like, but have struggled to find answers you could understand? Search no further! This book is the key to understanding more about God and what he wants from you. It is a must-read for anyone who has ever been curious about God and want answers that make sense."

—Jayson Samuels, co-founder NorthBridge Community Church, a strategic partnership of North Point Ministries

"More than just an expression, THE BIG GUY UPSTAIRS opens your heart and mind to the relevance of God, leaving a hunger and thirst that only He can satisfy. Rob had me laughing and crying as I recognized a piece of myself in each of these stories."

—Tim Popadic, speaker, author, community engagement innovator for DateNightWorks.com

THE BIG GUY UPSTAIRS

YOU, HIM,

AND HOW IT ALL WORKS

ROB STRONG

JERICHO
BOOKS ™

New York • Boston • Nashville

Out of a desire for privacy, brevity, clarity, or due to the faulty memory of the
author, some characters are composites and some names, personal details, and event
sequences have been modified.

All Scripture quotations, unless otherwise indicated, are taken from the Holy Bible,
New International Version®, NIV®. Copyright ©1973, 1978, 1984, 2011 by
Biblica, Inc.™ Used by permission of Zondervan. All rights reserved worldwide.
www.zondervan.com. The "NIV" and "New International Version" are trademarks
registered in the United States Patent and Trademark Office by Biblica, Inc.™

Scriptures noted NLT are from the Holy Bible, New Living Translation, copyright ©
1996. Used by permission of Tyndale House Publishers, Inc., Wheaton, Illinois
60189. All rights reserved.

Jericho Books
Hachette Book Group
237 Park Avenue
New York, NY 10017

JerichoBooks.com

Printed in the United States of America

RRD-C

First Edition: July 2013

10 9 8 7 6 5 4 3 2 1

This author is represented by Christopher Ferebee.

Jericho Books is an imprint of Hachette Book Group, Inc.
The Jericho Books name and logo are trademarks of Hachette Book Group, Inc.

The Hachette Speakers Bureau provides a wide range of authors for speaking events.
To find out more, go to www.HachetteSpeakersBureau.com or call (866) 376-6591.

The publisher is not responsible for websites (or their content) that are not owned by
the publisher.

Library of Congress Cataloging-in-Publication Data

Strong, Rob, 1971–
   The big guy upstairs : you, him, and how it all works / Rob Strong. — First edition
      pages cm.
   Summary: "As in the early works of Donald Miller, pastor Rob Strong uses
fascinating and humorous personal stories to offer a fresh perspective on how personal,
interactive, and relevant God can be in our lives." — Provided by publisher.
   ISBN 978-1-4555-2780-9 (hardback) — ISBN 978-1-4555-2781-6 (ebook)
   1. Spirituality. I. Title.
   BV4501.3.S787 2013
   248.4—dc23
                2013004820

CONTENTS

FOREWORD

Here's why I find this book so vital: Because Rob Strong is a pastor.

Now I realize that the word *pastor* is often not all that striking because there are lots of pastors out there. And that's true: there are lots of people who go by that title, a large number who have had the training, and many who hold that job.

But then there are the rare few who don't just hold the title of pastor; they *are* a pastor. It's a way they carry themselves, a manner of moving through the world that comes from somewhere deep in their bones. They embody—in some mysterious way that's hard to name but easy to spot when you see it—what it means to be the kind of person we look to for guidance in the things that matter most. They're the ones who carry themselves with a certain presence, with gravitas, and with authority—not in a heavy or oppressive or autocratic sort of way, but in a grounded, centered, calm-in-the-storm kind of way.

I've seen this happen with Rob countless times in our twenty years of friendship. We've been at events or meals or in conversations with people who Rob has just met, and I've watched as inevitably people begin to lean in and listen to him more and more intently, asking him questions, hanging on his words.

That's what happens when you're with him.

Now I realize that I'm dangerously close to coming off like a superfan or a promotional agent for all things ROB STRONG!!! But Rob has been a pastor to me on a number of occasions when I needed reminders and guidance and strength, and that's the sort of thing you just never forget.

Which brings me to this book.

I'm confident that you will find the guidance and strength and insight and wisdom here that Rob has been sharing with people for a number of years. He tells a number of stories about his life, stories that I've heard over the years and thought "If he were to write that down, I can't imagine how many people it would help..."

Which is what he's done here. So enjoy these words from a ... *pastor*.

Rob Bell

THE BIG GUY

UPSTAIRS

CHAPTER 0.5

PROXIMITY

I grew up in Minnesota, just outside of Minneapolis. I then attended college and graduate school just outside of Chicago. My first job as a pastor lasted thirteen years and was just outside of New York City. And now I am currently the lead pastor of a church just outside of Boston. If you were to assess me, you might think I like to be "just outside" of things. But the opposite is true. I love the richness of each of these cities and their surrounding towns.

There's also something I've experienced firsthand in my moves from Minneapolis to Chicago to New York to Boston: I've discovered that the farther east I move, the less religious people are. In fact, of the six states in New

England (Connecticut, Massachusetts, Rhode Island, Vermont, New Hampshire, and Maine), all are in the top-ten list of least-churched states in the country, according to Gallup polls. The top four are all in New England. This experience has given me insight into what I believe is the future spiritual landscape of the entire country. We are not growing more spiritual here in the United States. No, we are looking more and more like New England every single year. And to witness this genesis has helped me know better how to talk with people about God. And what is most interesting about this is that even if people are less religious, they are still quite spiritual. They believe in God. It's just not knowing what to do with that belief that leads them to me.

At a recent lunch with my friend Dave, he shared that he believes in God. So does his wife. But they don't really discuss it with each other, and certainly not with anyone else. Nor do they want to impose any set of beliefs on their kids about God. They don't go to church, and they don't plan to. They just want to be left alone to navigate these things on their own. But there is a problem with this that will only hurt them in the long run. Because when we don't connect with others or grow in more knowledge of God, we will gravitate toward some very generalized misconceptions about God. Namely that:

God is angry.

God is far away.

God doesn't care about us or the little things in our lives.

God is an unfair and revengeful judge.

God is just waiting for me to fail.

God is the faceless and uncaring Big Guy Upstairs.

I would propose to Dave and to you that these things are not true. In fact, I can't wait for you to see just who this amazing God really is.

Enjoy.

CHAPTER 1

PEACH TREES

S ometimes it takes years to discover what is right in front of your face.

The weather forecast for the Boston area was calling for freezing rain...in December. We usually expect snow during December, but rain? Doesn't rain just turn to snow when it's cold?

When it finally hit, the meteorologists weren't kidding. Up and down the north Atlantic coast, this "freezing rain" came in the night and rested upon our land. Having grown up in Minnesota and later living near Chicago and New York City, I had experienced ice storms before, but I had never, ever witnessed anything comparable to this. Nor had anyone else.

In the morning, I walked out and looked around at what seemed an almost apocalyptic landscape. Ice covered everything. Trees, huge trees, were contorted into eerie shapes and barely holding on to their branches. Cars were cocooned. Roads were now for skating, not driving. Nature had declared itself present and powerful.

More unique than the visual display, however, were the sounds, heard only in an event like this—the echoing sounds of ice moving and pulling and even breaking trees. I brought my four children gingerly out onto our deck. "Stop moving and stop talking. Just listen," I said. "You will never in your life hear this sound again." From every direction, the ice clicked, scratched, screamed in super-surround sound, almost surreal. And then...CRACK. A snapped tree limb. One after the other. Then whole trees crashed.

We lost power for five days and felt almost completely helpless. Months later, the cleanup was still going on, including the tree debris in my yard. We live on the side of one of several merging hills with many enormous and awkwardly situated trees. Some of the broken tree limbs were too difficult to move in the snowy winter, so we had to wait until spring to deal with them. One enormous, belligerent poplar that stands on the far edge of my yard still held a large, half-broken limb that refused to fall. I tried and tried, but I couldn't reach the crack with my tools, so I ultimately lowered my head, walked away, and conceded defeat. I knew this monster would eventually have to fall all on its own. It would only be a matter of time. I just needed to keep the family at a safe distance until it finally gave way. I was sure, based upon the significance of both the limb and the crack, that it would happen very soon.

But that poplar held on to its broken limb for years. As nature would have it, two and a half years later a hurricane hit our area. Yes, way up here. When Irene had finally blown over and moved on, I noticed that, among the many other limbs in my yard, that indefatigable poplar tree had finally relented and left its giant broken limb on the edge of my yard. It had put up an epic fight, but apparently even it could not allow that cracked branch to survive through a hurricane.

A few days later, I made my way over to move it. As I approached the limb, I noticed it sat parallel with the edge of the yard and a drop-off into the woods. At the edge of the grass is a twenty-foot drop almost straight down to the dark base of my property, which almost feels like an abyss. This tremendous, twenty-five-foot limb couldn't have fallen in a more perfect way. All I had to do was lift it from its middle point and toss it down the hill. Gravity would do its part and pull it out of sight. This would be easy.

As I positioned myself for the dead lift and big toss, I paused. I looked left and then right to make sure there were no obstacles in the way. And then I noticed it. There was an obstruction on the right. A weed. Rather, a giant weed. A weed the size of a small, seven-foot tree. You know weeds like this. They look tiny and harmless and you think, "I'll get to it soon," and then you get distracted and when you turn back, "Oh my," you swear, "it grew a few feet!" This was one of those weeds.

The weed-tree was an obstacle and unwelcome growth. However, I realized that if I did this limb-throw correctly, I could simultaneously crush the weed and get the super limb to the bottom of the hill. "You're gonna get it, weed-tree. You're going down," I said aloud.

I lifted. I looked at that weed-tree one more time. "Your days of uglifying my yard are done, weed. May the weight of this limb break you to pieces."

And then...What the? Something was flashing through the windblown leaves.

I set the limb back down and looked carefully at that weed-tree again. The flash was not reflective, but it offered a glimpse of color. I approached it, stepping off my lawn into knee-high weeds, and reached out, carefully lifting back some of the leaves. And what I found behind those leaves, upon closer inspection, were thirty to forty of the most hidden but also the most beautiful peaches I had ever seen. Not what I ever expected to find on my property. There, growing just beyond the edge of my lawn, surrounded by leaves, low-lying weeds, and briars, was a peach tree.

I stood motionless. Were these really peaches? Here, north of Boston, in my woods? I realized I had never really seen a peach tree before. I wasn't completely sure what I was looking at. "Susan! Come over here. You have to see this!" I called to my wife who was working in the garage. "I think I'm going crazy!"

From the sound of the urgency in my voice, she responded quickly. I could see her looking at me from a distance with a quizzical expression on her face. "What's wrong?" she yelled. My four-year-old daughter was trotting behind her also wanting to see what was going on.

"Nothing is wrong," I said. "But I am incredibly confused." I pointed at the tree. "Is this what I think it is?" I asked, intentionally not giving her my diagnosis when Susan stood beside me, looking at what was now, possibly, a peach tree.

"That's a peach tree," she said to the tree. "On our property." Then she looked at me and said, "Here, north of Boston? Who? What? How?"

I reached over and gently picked one of the peaches from the tree. At the grocery store you squeeze fruit like you know what you're doing, but you really don't. I did that to the peach. But as I cradled it in my hands, I knew this peach was supposed to be picked that day. It was exactly what you imagine it should feel like in the grocery store. It was perfect.

"Here, try it," I said.

"I'm not trying it . . . You try it."

"No, you," I said, offering her the peach, hoping she would take it.

"What if there's bugs or worms in it? Or what if it gets me sick? It hasn't been treated," she argued.

The curiosity was killing me. "Forget it, I'm gonna try it." I brought the peach to my mouth and took a bite of the most delicious, most incredible, most flavorful, most wonderful peach I have ever tasted.

Because I didn't drop into convulsions, Susan was satisfied there were no bugs. She took a bite and agreed that it was amazingly tasty. My youngest took a bite too. As juices dripped down her chin, she said, "Oh, wow!"

This was no weed. It certainly wasn't a weed-tree. It wasn't a nuisance. This was a treasure. And, for the record, I did not throw the limb on it.

Immediately, Susan abandoned her work in the garage and spent the next several hours clearing all the thorn bushes, vines, and weeds from the peach tree that stood just off our lawn in the weeds and on the top edge of the hill. This incredible discovery was something worth investing in and caring for. She stood in poison ivy, she cut her hands, she sweated crazily because the peach tree was completely worth it. She intentionally cared for a tree of such great value.

As I stood at a distance and watched her work around the peach tree, this occurred to me: How long has God stood just beyond the edge of my lawn, like that peach tree, and I've not known it? How long have I relegated God to the distant part of my life? How long has he been pushed into the weeds with thorns and vines as I ignored him? How long have I walked through life knowing the Big Guy was upstairs, but convinced I didn't need him?

And to you, how long have you had God on the very edge of your life? How long has he been pushed to a place that it is difficult to remember him? How long has he been out of your life that you don't know the value of even knowing him?

I know there are times over the years that I've let God remain on the edges of my life, amidst the weeds. I've forgotten just how amazing he is. And I've even struggled to understand the value of knowing him. Yes, I am a pastor, but like you, I am a self-reliant being who places God at the outside of my life.

But what if we could approach God as Susan and I did that peach tree and gently push back a few of the leaves? What if we could discover that God is not what we thought, but better than we ever imagined? What if this God has been right in front of us all along? And what if approaching that tree is the best decision you ever made?

What if?

CHAPTER 2

THE ULTIMATE PARTY STOPPER

With some reflective thinking and some deep soul-searching, I've discovered I am the ultimate party stopper.

We were celebrating the Fourth of July at a friend's house. Susan, the kids, and I were having a great time. We weren't familiar with anyone except our dear friends, the hosts. Having a job like mine, sometimes knowing no one at a social gathering is just fine. As a pastor from a nearby town, none of these people knew me or what I did for a living and therefore didn't treat me differently. Once in a while that is a liberating feeling, to be able to sit around the outdoor fire with a glass of wine, next to the pool, with people I've been laughing with for hours who don't know me from Adam. I'm just another guy. Maybe even a funny guy. A guy someone would like to hang with. I was feeling pretty good.

And then came the fatal moment. The lady across the fire pit voiced The Question. "Hey, Rob . . . what do you do for a living?"

Having been in situations like this before, I realized immediately that much of the equilibrium of the night was going to hang on my answer. Tell them I'm in sales and the music keeps thumping, people keep laughing, and the fun keeps flowing. Tell them I'm a manager at a nearby business and they'll probably not remember my answer the next morning.

"Well, now that's a good question." I was buying some time.

I carefully thought through my answer. I'm not afraid to admit I'm a pastor. Nor am I ashamed of what I do or teach or stand for. No, I'm not hesitant for those reasons. Rather, I am fully aware that my truthful answer could literally change the entire rhythm of the party. It might even redirect an hour or two of discussion and put me, or "what I do," at the center. It often seems to do that. But did I want that on this particular night? Did I want to bring my occupation into this moment?

I also knew I didn't want to lie. And I didn't want to hide. So I finally confessed, "I'm a pastor."

And everything went silent.

When I reveal my profession here in the northeastern part of the United States, it usually prompts a unique initial reaction: confusion—because most people here don't understand what "pastor" means. They either do not attend a church or they have a Roman Catholic heritage (55–60 percent of the population), so there is often a pause and a look of bewilderment upon my news. One of the first questions asked is how a "priest" could have a wife and kids. "How can you be married as a priest?" It is then that I begin to explain that I'm not a Roman Catholic priest but a Protestant pastor. Again, confusion and bewilderment. "What's that?" and "That's a job?" I assure them that, indeed, it is a real job.

On this particular July night, this perfect night, after midnight, my kids asleep in their friends' bedrooms upstairs, fire going, people laughing, music thumping, my answer "I'm a pastor" did exactly what I feared it would. It brought that entire section of the party to a deafening halt. I could feel car tires screeching the way they do when they have to stop instantly from a full-speed charge. This party around the fire had stopped. Again, I was the ultimate party stopper.

"A pastor?"

"You're a what?"

"A what?"

I could see my fellow partiers trying to piece this reality together. I had seen it before in other settings. In their minds, it goes something like this: "He's a man who works at a church...a man of the cloth? Oh my God...what did I say earlier tonight? What stories did I tell? What language did I use? How do I talk now? What do I say? What do I not say?"

There was a floating feeling of awkwardness in the air.

I could see their minds working through the files of their brains, trying to remember the past four to five hours. Had they offended me? And, if so, had they also offended God? Eventually someone usually says something like, "Really? Wow. You work for the Big Guy Upstairs? Now that's different." And then come the questions about where I work, what exactly I do, and do I like it.

The party had shifted and become a bit uncomfortable, but interestingly, I noticed that it wasn't a bad shift for some. In fact, the night had possibly just become a bit more interesting for them. Others weren't sure what to do. It was like revealing a pet snake in the middle of a group of people. Some get close and pet it and inquire about its name. Some jump back in fear. Some stand carefully at a safe distance and observe. That's how it is for me in settings like these: I get a variety of reactions.

On this particular night, this perfect night, however, there was an unexpected turn of events. After a few people wandered back into the house to another section of the party, those who stayed engaged with me in discussion. The laughter and looseness of the party around the pool had changed, but the ensuing discussion about faith, religion, God, and beliefs was one for the ages. Yes, the ultimate party stopper shook the original party, but a new party had begun, and it was actually pretty cool. And pretty revealing.

By revealing, I mean that in this setting a clear reality about people and our culture started to become obvious to me. The questions came slowly at first, but then took off—so many questions. That's true of our culture, isn't it? We question anything and everything. We accept very little with blind faith. Maybe years ago we trusted the company that said it had our best interest in mind while they were pouring toxic chemicals into the ground or a river nearby. Maybe years ago we trusted politicians who promised they would make a difference, but who ultimately sold themselves out for personal gain. Maybe decades ago that pastor or priest was trusted as good and wise in a community, but that was lost through TV scandals, accusations of inappropriate behavior, and money and sex. Maybe years ago we trusted policemen, teachers, neighbors, friends, but that gap between ourselves and others is filled less with trust and more with doubt these days.

And the doubt and hesitancy we feel in our culture toward these things only shifts to trust when we have an opportunity to ask some questions. We ask to determine whether we can trust. And that's not bad. We build much of our trust through questioning.

My new acquaintances that evening were no exception. They had a person of "religion" sitting right in front of them, and the questions that had been simmering in their heads for a long time could now finally be asked. I think about it this way: If I need my computer fixed, I don't go to the Foot Locker. If I need new running shoes, I don't go to the Apple Store. When questions come to mind about God, you can't expect to get answers from your waiter or your dentist or your grocer. No, it's not very often that one gets to sit with a pastor and fire away theological and spiritual questions.

So they did. And they weren't asking trivia like, "Hey, what's the deal with that guy who was eaten by a whale?" Or, "Seriously, how big was that ark?" No, these were questions educated, intelligent, and skeptical people ask in our culture today. There was meat hanging from their inquiries.

"Do you really believe there is a God? Because I don't."

"How can you believe we were created by a God?"

"How has religion created anything but pain and wars over the centuries?"

"Don't you think religion is useless?"

"How can you make a living doing that job?"

"What is it, again, that you actually do?"

Those were the warm-ups. Then the queries grew more interesting...

"What is the point of life?"

"What does God want with us?"

"Does God get angry with me?"

"How do I know God is listening?"

"Can I have a conversation with God?"

"What am I supposed to do if there is a God?"

"If God is loving, then why are there _____?"

And on and on into the night, and we just kept adding wood to the fire (pun quite intended).

In their questions I could see their spiritual beliefs rising to the surface. There seemed to be a common theme. Most everyone had some element of belief in a God, some concept of him or at least a "higher power." But none of them really knew what God was actually like. They knew there was a God, but he was out of reach. God was that peach tree on the edge of their lawn, with weeds growing all around and through it. They had no idea what to do to bring God in closer, close enough so they could figure it all out.

They were like people touching a statue in the dark and trying to guess what it is. There was no consistency. No clear image. No idea how God worked or interacted with people. No general consensus on God or heaven or death or the church. Just hunches and speculation based on smatterings of their various church backgrounds, readings they'd picked up in bookstores or perused on the Internet, and unexplainable or even painful life experiences.

The more I listened, the more I realized the reason there were so many questions and opinions was not only because we are inclined as a culture to question, but because of a consistent antagonism or a clear sense of apathy toward organized religion. That gap between people and religion is not filled with trust. So, on that perfect night, the partiers had the chance to ask what was burning in their hearts. They wanted to know more about the Big Guy Upstairs and how he fit into the bigger picture of life. They wanted to bring him out of the weeds.

Maybe this resonates with you a little. Many say, "I believe in a 'god.' And I also have many questions about this 'god.' But I don't trust the church or anyone enough to get answers, so I will continue to speculate, mostly on my own."

I get that.

When one has a question about God or Jesus or spiritual matters, it's good to spend time with someone who studies and teaches on that topic for a living. I sensed that's what people were feeling that night. As I've thought more about that night and similar experiences I've had, I've discovered a few things.

First, we do want answers. Simple, logical, clear, "Oh, that makes sense" answers. We question, but in that cloud of confusion, we all would like things spelled out and clarified, especially about something as philosophical or ethereal as God.

Second, we want those answers without arrogance. We want someone to lay out simple truth but not tell it or preach it or order it. We want it revealed to us so that it makes sense and that we're brought in on that revelation.

Several years ago, I found myself in an odd situation. I was hanging out with a friend at his house when he said his dad, Howard, was going to stop over for a bit too. I met his dad for the first time that day. He was not a big man, but was certainly gruff, tough, and looked weathered. I was certain that this sixty-five-year-old guy had truly earned his way through life. If the phrase "man's man" was in the dictionary, this guy's picture was beside the definition.

After just a few minutes of small talk between the three of us, my friend unexpectedly received a phone call that removed him from the room for a while. Here sat this rugged guy alone with the pastor, except he didn't know that. Howard started fast and asked, "So, what do you do?"

"I'm a pastor," I replied rather matter-of-factly.

"You work for the Big Guy Upstairs, huh? Geez, I don't believe any of that God-and-Jesus crap anyway." He said "God and Jesus" as one word. "And I hate the church."

That didn't make me feel at ease. This could go really bad really fast. "Me too," I said.

"What? You work for the church, and you hate the church?"

"Well, I don't know about 'hate,' but there are many things about the church that trouble me."

"Like what?"

I sensed Howard was genuinely curious about this paradox. I looked at him, eyeball to eyeball, and said, "I don't like the emphasis on rules or perfect behavior. And I don't like the self-righteousness that the church and its people can give off. I struggle with the way the church gives the appearance that it has it all together, and yet at the same time there are many societal ills that are ongoing and unchanging. These are a few of the things I don't like about the church."

Silence for a few seconds. Then he looked at me and asked, "Then what the hell are you a pastor for?"

"Because I don't think God has always been pleased with the church either. From what I've studied and read in the Bible, Jesus came to challenge the ideas and practices of religion. He was persecuted and eventually put to death for the way he challenged the religious elite. I believe in God enough to try and share that message in spite of the church. I try to have my church step beyond the rules and into a healthy relationship with God."

"I thought Jesus was all about setting up religious rules. Didn't he start the church?"

"No. He didn't. In fact, his passion wasn't setting up a church system or establishing new rules or forcing anyone into anything. Rather, he came here to this earth to share something with us."

"What?"

"That although it seems like God is incredibly far away and comes off as 'The Big Guy Upstairs,' he is actually very close and very interested in you as a person. He cares about you."

My new friend said nothing.

I deduced it wasn't that Howard didn't believe in God; it's that he didn't believe in a God who was associated with all the bad he believed the church to be. If the only choices were to either believe in the God of the church as he knew it or to not believe in God, he would choose the latter, not the former. If church was the tollbooth on the highway to God, then he would take the back roads.

"Let me ask you something, Howard. Do you really not believe in God? Or is it the church you're really not believing in?" I wanted to ask him about his childhood church experience because I sensed that was where the issue lay. But as it turned out, I didn't need to.

He paused before he answered. Maybe ten seconds went by. "If there is a God," he said, "he can't be from the intimidating and guilt-inducing church I grew up in. I hated the church my parents made me attend. They didn't even go themselves—they just dropped me off at the door on Sunday mornings and drove off. I was never good enough there. I hated that church."

There it was. Howard didn't disbelieve there was a God. To him, God was so entangled in the knots of an unhealthy church experience that he couldn't connect to God. He hadn't thrown out God entirely; it was just easier to ignore God, push him to the outer edges of his life.

Through all the clutter and haze of many messages about God, there are revelations about God that are true and good, yet simple and direct. God is that peach tree in the distance. God can be approached and examined and even experienced. God doesn't force himself into our lives, he simply desires for us to discover him. And when we do, it is amazing. This God is not irrelevant or angry or impotent or lost or uncaring or vengeful or faraway upstairs. No, God wants to reveal himself to you in new and incredible ways. He is the peach tree on the edge of your life, waiting to be discovered.

CHAPTER 3

BROWN SHOES

When I was less than a year old, my father and mother divorced.

I'm told it was a traumatic event, but I was too young to know. A few years later, my mom remarried a wonderful man to whom she is still married today. My new stepfather chose to invest in my sister and me as if we were his own children. From the time I was four years old, he was my dad. He was there through all of my life and never, ever shirked the responsibility. He shaped me through his character, his high ethics, and most of all, the model of how he loved my mom and God. He continues to do so to this day. He is truly a hero in my life.

In addition to my stepfather's presence, however, I also

had my biological father in my life. But that has always been, and continues to be, a very difficult and strained relationship. Growing up, my biological "dad" and I talked on the phone weekly and I would visit on certain holidays and in the summers. He lived two states away, so visits involved a long, eight-hour drive each way. As one might expect, it was hard to develop the relationship. And I struggled to know how to fit him into my life in a growing or significant way. And that troubled him too. In fact, it troubled him so much that he took umbrage with my relationship with my stepfather and my mother. He saw me as being too close to them, and thus he felt he was being discarded. I don't think, being a kid, I could completely comprehend what he was implying, but as I look back, I can see the guilt that was put upon me and I can now see how the resentment grew and grew in him. But it wasn't clear to me then. That is, until I received a long and unexpected letter during my freshman spring finals week in college that told me he didn't want to be my father anymore. He said he was done with the games, done with the frustration he felt, and he wanted to end the relationship permanently. When I turned to the final page of the letter, I could barely make out his last words through the blur of my tears.

"Signed, Your Former Dad."

I remember exactly where I was standing as I read that letter.

I was looking out of my dorm-room window on a cloudy May afternoon. I struggled to comprehend what I had just read, and I didn't know what to do. I certainly didn't understand his reasoning. And with those tears came small trickles of anger in my heart. I don't think I knew it then, but I can see it now as I look back. Anger and pain mixed together like water and mud that became quietly and imperceptibly packed hard around my heart. I just didn't know it at the time.

Silence from my dad became my new reality. For the next thirteen years, he never called or initiated any contact. Water and mud, anger and pain, continued to mix and dry together. My heart was shifting ever so slowly, ever so quietly. Through Susan's encouragement, I wrote twice—in years two and three—but his short responses came in the mail as reiterations of his initial statement: "My feelings are the same, so there won't be a relationship." Anger became my new reality. I could not grasp his logic. And that became profoundly clearer with the birth of each of my own children. "How could a father abandon his child?" I would ask myself.

But something happened during the next ten years of silence. I grew more and more numb to the situation and felt I was less overtly angry. In fact, I believed that I had grown to accept the whole situation. I managed to block it out, stuff it away, and even at times forgot about it. My biological father was not my dad anymore, and I moved forward. On occasion, someone would ask me about my past, and when I told the story, I could routinely hit the high points quite unemotionally. And because of the numbness, it didn't really feel like it was my story anymore. It felt more like I was recounting a movie I had seen on an old "after-school special." It didn't seem to faze me.

However, after thirteen years of fatherly silence and now serving as a pastor, I was coming up on a new four-week teaching series on forgiveness. What I didn't expect to happen was what happened on the Wednesday before I began the first teaching. My dear friend Tim asked me what I would be speaking on that coming Sunday. I quickly explained the intent of the whole series and that we would start with asking people to confront the issue of forgiveness in their own lives, asking them to consider who they were currently in conflict with. When I was done, he asked me a most unexpected question. He said, "Rob, if you're teaching a series on forgiveness, you need to make sure it's also true for you. So I should ask you, do you have any unresolved conflict in your own life?"

Wow, I wasn't expecting that, but the question made sense. If I was going to teach my congregation these things, then they needed to be things I had wrestled with too. Otherwise, who was I to teach it? So I thought long and hard about it, even tilting my head upward and placing my hand on my chin. "No. I don't have any conflict that I can think of," I responded quite matter-of-factly.

Tim, unfortunately for me, is a licensed therapist. "Rob, there must be something. I know you're not thinking hard enough about this."

I sat still. I started to mentally walk through the name and face of each person in my life. "No, I can't think of anyone right now that I am harboring anger toward or them toward me."

"Go back a bit further, Rob. Anyone you've cut out of your life? Anyone you're blocking emotions from because they've hurt you so deeply?" Tim knew exactly where he was driving because I had told him my life story and shared, very matter-of-factly, that my biological father had disowned me years earlier.

And then it hit me.

Like a truck with no brakes hitting a wall, I felt myself mentally smash. Tim told me later he could see the realization hit me physically. I felt myself trying to stop the flow of emotions that had been locked away so deeply. I stammered, paused, teared up, and was confused. My father had been locked away in my private closet for years. I could tell "the story" to anyone. In a very surface way I could share about this dad I once knew, as if he wasn't real and it never REALLY happened. But in this moment with Tim, I reached back to a place I hadn't visited in years, pulled him out from the depths of my mind and heart, and acknowledged him as real. Facing this emotional and un-resolved relationship, after all of these years, didn't go over very easily.

Tim looked at me and waited for me to settle a bit. But he wasn't done. "Rob, you need to call him."

My eyes blew open. Anger shot through every part of me. "No way, Tim!"

"Rob, you need to call him."

"Tim, you don't understand." I was contorting in my chair. I was so uncomfortable. I wanted to run out of the room. But I had enough years of meeting with people and talking with them about their family dynamics to know, deep down, that I did need to face this nightmare if I was ever going to be truly free. When I was a child, I used to dread going to the dentist to get a cavity filled. I had to go or eventually the tooth would rot away. My unresolved and locked-away problems with my dad had to be addressed, even if I absolutely didn't want to.

"Rob, you know what I'm saying is true. You are teach-ing an entire series on forgiveness in relationships to many, many people. Yet you have an enormous, unresolved re-lationship in your own life. There is conflict deep within you that you are hiding from. And if you didn't know it, but I'm sure you do, it is affecting you and how you live and how you interact with your own children. How can you get up in front of your people and teach about their need to work through their conflicts if you're not facing your own issues?"

I really didn't like Tim at that moment. Not one bit. But I knew he was right. I nodded.

I knew I had to face this fear of reconnecting with my dad. And that's exactly what it was. A fear. What specific fear was so potent and powerful and paralyzing for me? Rejection. I played through the scenario in my head a dozen times before I recognized it. I imagined myself walking up to his front door and knocking. I could see him in my mind's eye opening up the door, looking surprised to see me, and then saying, "I told you before, I'm not your dad. I haven't changed my mind. Leave." That scenario had kept me from trying to reconcile with him. I didn't think I could face that level of rejection again. It's easier to just hide and hold back than to deal with it.

Because it's not just any rejection. This would be from my dad. My father. It's different when it's Dad. I've been rejected by girls in my dating years. I've been rejected in job offers. But a parent's rejection cuts deeper than any other rejection on earth, simply because they are your mom or dad.

My earthly estranged father was my biggest problem that day of self-discovery. Tim had unearthed a personal nightmare in my life and left me to do something about it. So that same day, after I had calmed down a bit, I built up the resolve I needed to do exactly what Tim said I needed to do. I needed to call my dad. I walked over to my computer and began a search for him. The Internet is sometimes too powerful in this respect. I soon discovered that he and his wife no longer lived in the town where he had lived for thirty-five years, but had moved out West and built a home on the side of a mountain on the outskirts of a small town. I deduced all this within ten minutes of searching and even found his phone number.

With my hand shaking, I picked up the receiver and began to dial. My heart was pounding, and my stomach felt ill. After three rings, his wife answered. I identified who I was. Silence.

Then she said, "Wow, Robby, this is quite a shock." Again, silence. But then she said, "How are you?"

A tiny sense of relief began to come over me. At least she wasn't shutting me down. "I'm doing fine. I'm married now. I have two children. Another one on the way." Every word was shaky. I sounded like a slightly warped record on an old record player.

"I assume you're looking for your father," she finally said.

"Yes. I wanted to touch base with him. Is he around?"

"You know what, Robby? He's going to be a bit taken aback by your call. Could you give me an hour to get him prepped and then call back?" She was kind and thinking clearly.

"Yes, no problem. An hour. I'll call then. Good-bye."

Waiting an hour was not a "no-problem" proposition. It had taken all of my courage to call the first time. Now I had to wait. Not easy.

But I did. When I called again, his wife answered—again. This time, however, I could hear him in the background calling his dog. The mere sound of his voice shook me. It didn't matter that I hadn't talked with him for thirteen years. It didn't matter that he had left my mom and my sister and me. It didn't matter that he really was a difficult person to connect with. He was my dad, and that couldn't be denied. No matter how old a father or mother gets (or the child, correspondingly), they are still your father or mother. They are a significant presence in your life. Hearing my dad's voice in the distance through the phone line reminded me of this truth.

"Hello?" he said after his wife handed him the phone. It was not a hostile "hello." Nor an angry "hello." It was a "hello" from an elderly man who might not have the best hearing anymore. It was a strained "hello."

"Hello . . . Dad?" Again, the voice shaking and the racing heart.

"Well, hello, Rob." Still, no anger. But the potential for rejection still hung in the air. "What's going on?"

"Well, Dad, I'm calling because we haven't talked in thirteen years. And...well...I didn't think that was right. I felt that we should at least connect a bit again."

Silence. Then, "Hmmm. All right." He didn't sound convinced, but added, "So what are you doing with your life these days?"

The door opened just a bit. Rejection didn't rain down, and anger didn't burst forth.

I had many, many questions for him that day, but most of it went unsaid, like: Why did you leave our family? And why would you write a letter like that? What were you thinking? Why would you let thirteen years go by and not want to reconnect with your son? I had so many questions, but at this point, just breaking the ice seemed to matter the most.

And because of that phone call, a first, clear step toward each other was taken, which meant it was one step in the opposite direction of the many years of estrangement. We talked about his retirement and his move to a new state. I talked of the wife and children I now had and the activities they were involved in. It was a conversation that just days before I had thought would have been impossible. But it wasn't. We were actually talking. I struggled to believe it. Not that the anger disappeared—for either of us—but it was a start.

Unfortunately, though, the relationship hasn't progressed much more since that phone call some nine years ago. We e-mail each other about once a month, but it never has much substance, even if I ask for more. I have invited him to visit my family, but he refuses. I have invited him to meet me in a neutral place, but he refuses. And I have even offered to go visit him where he is, but he refuses. And when he signs his e-mails to me now, he signs with his name, not as "Dad." I don't understand it, but I've come to accept it. I've even come to a point of forgiving him, but sometimes I wonder if I'm really that far. And it is absolutely clear to me that I don't have a healthy and good picture of what a "father" is from this man. He is not the model for it. And that affects me as a dad myself.

As much as I would like to say it doesn't, it does. And that is because no matter how estranged or distant we are, we're still father and son, whether we admit it or not. We are bound together by blood and by emotions. My relationship with my stepfather is very positive, but my association with "father" from a biological standpoint is very negative. The contrast is significant. And it can make it difficult to fully trust and embrace God as my heavenly father.

GOD AS FATHER

Which leads me to Jesus.

One of the primary words Jesus chose to describe God

was the word "Father." In addition, he made sure that everyone around him understood God from that perspective too. He used "Father" to describe God while he talked with his disciples and when he spoke to crowds of people. But probably the most obvious moment came when he was teaching a large gathering of people how to pray. Christians today call it "The Lord's Prayer." And when Jesus began, he started it like this, "Our Father, who is in heaven..." (see Matthew 6:9).

Jesus' word "Father" is a volatile word for me. It represents both good and bad things in my life.

And I'm clearly not alone. When you use the "father" word in our culture, it stirs up a spectrum of emotions, both good and bad. It can make it incredibly difficult for people to connect positively to God if they don't trust even the idea of a "father" in their own lives. Abandonment, abuse, anger, guilt, pain. If that's the lens you look through, then you might ask, "What was Jesus thinking?"

I've wrestled with that very lens in my own life. With much time and study and consideration, I have concluded that when Jesus called God "our Father," he was intentionally revealing a picture of a father in the most beautiful and healthy sense of the word. He was describing a father who doesn't disengage. Nor does he detach, stand afar, and just watch. He doesn't abandon, hurt, abuse, or take advantage of his children. And God, as father, doesn't use guilt and shame as a motivator. In contrast, Jesus is describing the healthiest imaginable form of father who instead chooses to empower, interact with, and invest in his children. He also understands, empathizes, and wants a deep and relevant relationship with each of us. Fathers in our culture can appear to be detached and aloof, but those are never the models of a healthy father. God, on the other hand, has all the markings of a true and good father. Look at these very beautiful examples found in the Bible:

> How great is the love the Father has lavished on us, that we should be called children of God! And that is what we are.
>
> 1 John 3:1

> I will be a Father to you, and you will be my sons and daughters, says the Lord Almighty.
>
> 2 Corinthians 6:18

So why would Jesus use that word to describe God? Because it captures the essence of God—God's heart and how he wants to be in our lives. Intimately. Closely. He wants to be involved and invested in the way a father is involved and invested in the lives of his children. It isn't by accident that Jesus uses "father" to describe God.

It is, instead, by design.

But embracing that design isn't easy. And not only because we may have misconstrued images of our own fathers tainting our understanding of our heavenly father, but because the idea of God as intimate and close and being interested in my daily life is also difficult for me to embrace. In fact, for some, the idea that God is close enough to be present around us is hard enough to process.

THE LAMP THAT NEVER SHOOK

These philosophical wrestlings came early for me. As a teenager, I would sometimes lie in bed and question the existence of God. The whole story of God and Jesus almost felt like a grand fairy tale. A man born of a virgin woman? The blind able to see again? The deaf able to hear again? Feeding thousands with only a few loaves of bread and several fish? How could it be true? And a God who is the creator of the universe and all that it holds and who also claims to have an eternal presence? That seemed farfetched for me. I decided that I wanted some empirical evidence. So I would stare directly at the lamp on top of my dresser and say into the air around me, "God, if you're really real, then make my lamp shake." I would say it again and again. And I would wait. And wait.

And the lamp never shook.

Even though it didn't shake, I still wasn't ready to give up entirely. And that is because of one question that kept coming back to my mind over and over: "If there is no God, then what started it all?" I mean, even if science declared the "Big Bang" theory a fact, something had to create the bang. It goes against all the laws of physics to declare that, in just this one instance, something came from nothing and that something could move or ignite on its own. And the start of the universe is no small event to simply gloss over. After thinking it over, I eventually decided that it would take entirely more effort for me to accept this dichotomy as fact than to accept that the only thing that could start all things ... was God. So I chose to accept that there was a God, even if he didn't shake my lamp when I asked.

But accepting the existence of God is one thing. Experiencing him throughout life, especially in the small matters, is another. If we accept that there is a God who created all things but we stop there, then something interesting happens to our perception of God. He ultimately ends up at the edge of our lawns. He is forgotten; he's not our intimate and close father. We don't know what to do with him, so we avoid him. And I felt myself doing just that. Sure, I accepted the idea of God for the reasons above, but I didn't know what to do with him beyond that. And for me, that didn't sit right. So that led me to a second question: "If there is a God, then what did he create us for?" Or, in other words, what does he want with us? I kept thinking through that question and concluded that if you could answer it, you will have figured out the most overlooked but most important piece of information in the entire world.

So I came to the conclusion that although he didn't shake my desktop lamp, God was so deeply interested in me that he wanted me to know him as my heavenly father. And I began to embrace that idea. It felt good and right. And the more I plumbed the depths of that word "father," I also discovered that my heavenly father wanted to interact with me. He wanted to talk with me and have me trust in him. And I discovered that I can even ask him for something I need.

It took me many years to discover and embrace that concept—that God had significant interest in me—and it took the actions of my own father, who decided early on that he wanted nothing to do with me, for me to finally see it.

Jesus was intentional in using the word "father" because he knew that not only is it a potent and volatile word, but alongside "mother," "father" is one of the most powerful words describing an enormous role of responsibility. My ongoing experience with my earthly biological father, and his rejection of me, has revealed to me that there is power in that title. It goes way beyond a name. And it is deeper than "somebody up there." It certainly runs in contrast to the concept of God as the distant Big Guy Upstairs—this impersonal and all-knowing being.

What is so fascinating to me about all of this is that God volunteered to take the role of "father" upon himself. When my stepfather married my mom, he knew he would also be shouldering the responsibility of two young children. And he welcomed that responsibility. God is the same way. "Bring it on," God says. Give me that title. I want it. In fact, I want to not only be known as your father, I want to be known as the great and beautiful and good father who loves his children and cares for them. "I will never leave you nor forsake you," God tells us (see Joshua 1:5). Yes, he welcomes everything that comes with being known as "father."

And that is my point about God. God didn't reveal himself to us through the Bible as "The Boss." Or the "Big Guy Upstairs." Or as comedian Dane Cook calls him, "Mr. Big Guns." When he told us he was our Father, he was making it clear that he wanted to take upon himself ALL the responsibility and consequences and import that go with that title. That role, as our heavenly parent, is the most important and, at the same time, most intimate role he could possibly have chosen. It is so intimate that he even cares about the small and seemingly insignificant things in our lives. He knows of our struggles and our problems. He is fully cognizant of our foibles and even our wants and needs.

Including the little things—like a pair of shoes.

BROWN SHOES

After we had our first child, one particular reality was difficult to swallow—converting from a D.I.N.K. (double-income-no-kids) couple to a one-income family. Obviously, things started to get tight for us financially.

If you have had this happen to you, you know this new reality: you look in the mirror and realize, sadly, that you're really not looking cool in those old pants, sad shirt, and not-so-groovy shoes. Overnight you've become the very person you vowed you'd never become—the fashion-challenged parents who raised you. Suddenly you're not "with it." And you're without the money to do much about it. I'm not complaining, but let's face facts: the family thing is a life-changing reality. Including how you look.

With that as the backdrop, you'll understand why I was frustrated about my shoes. My brown shoes. I was living a very simple shoe life. One pair of running shoes. One pair of black shoes. And one pair of brown shoes. The problem was my brown shoes were not only getting old and worn, they were also hideous. I was embarrassed every time I wore them out of the house. One reason they looked so bad was that money had been tight, and I had cut corners. These shoes had been purchased from a cheaper chain store, from the all-sales-are-final rack. And now they were way past their prime. My mom used to tell me that when you cut corners with clothes and shoes, you get what you pay for. I was paying for it, for months.

So I began to save a few bucks on the side.

When I had saved enough, I decided I was going to do it right and buy a good pair of shoes. A nice pair of brown shoes. I even prayed about it because I knew that things were tight and I wanted this to be a wise purchase. I was now feeling right about this timing. Yes, I was going to buy me some new shoes. New brown shoes. I was going to spend that little extra to get the right brown shoes.

On the eve of the brown-shoe-purchase, I smiled. I went to bed smiling, for I was going to buy some new brown shoes the next afternoon. Would you believe that three times that night I woke up and then remembered, each time, that I was going to buy some new brown shoes? Oh yes.

In the morning, I felt pretty good. It was going to be a glorious day. As I was putting the extra pillows up on the bed, my wife asked me what I was up to that day. I didn't miss a beat. Tossing another pillow on the bed, "Baby," I said with a smile, "I'm buying me some new brown shoes today." And off to work I went with a plan to duck out of the office a bit early and find the brown shoes later that afternoon.

After a busy morning, I had an appointment with a friend scheduled for just after lunch. He was a pastor in a town about forty-five minutes away, and we were going to catch up on some ministry ideas. I saw him as he pulled into our church parking lot. Hopping out of his little red pickup truck, he stood out. He's at least 6'3" and one of the thinnest people you'll ever meet. His dreadlocks bounced as he crossed toward the church. He's also the lead singer in a band. He stinks of cool. He is cool defined. Black leather jacket, the right jeans, etc. Cool-in-motion.

We talked for about an hour. After that, as I started to walk him out of our facility, he turned and asked, "Hey, Rob, what size shoe do you wear?"

"Huh?"

"It's just a question, bro. What size is your foot?"

I told him as we arrived at the door. I suddenly remembered something in my office I had forgotten to give him. "Can you come back to my office for a second?" I asked.

I sat down and rummaged through a drawer in my desk as he sat back down in the chair across from me with my desk separating us. As I was digging, I felt a hard hit on

my leg under my desk. I looked up to see my friend staring at me.

"Dude, try on my shoe."

I looked down at my ugly brown shoes, and there was
one of his shoes lying next to them.

That was the first time in my adult life I had ever had
an individual ask me to try on their shoe. If something was
not cool, it was that. I looked down at the shoe. Then back
at him. Then down at the shoe, hesitating.

"It's new. I bought them two days ago. Just try it on."

Okay, that was a bit better—it was a new shoe. So I
slipped off my shoe and proceeded to put his on. It fit...
perfectly. I looked up at him and said, "Yeah, it's a good
shoe." I leaned over and started to take it off when I felt
something hit me in the legs again. It was his other shoe.

"Here, put that one on too."

At this point I was really confused and, honestly, a bit
concerned about why he was throwing his shoes at me and
asking me to try them on. But being a friend, I trusted
him and I pulled it on. He asked me to walk around a bit.
I did.

"How do they feel?" he asked like a shoe salesman.

"Good," I responded. They actually felt great. A perfect
fit. I then sat back down and looked at him, unsure of what
was going on.

Before I could ask where he bought them or tell him

I was going shopping for new shoes that afternoon, my friend deliberately leaned forward and said, "Rob, do you have any idea why, during my entire forty-five minute drive over here to meet with you today, God kept telling me, 'Give Rob your shoes, give Rob your shoes, give Rob your shoes'? What was up with that?"

I froze. And I was speechless. It was an incredibly awkward but stunning moment. I looked down at the perfect, brown shoes upon my feet and looked back up at him. I then stammered, "Well, you see...I have terrible shoes. That is, terrible brown shoes, and, um, I was going to go get new ones today." I sat there staring and thinking for a moment, then matter-of-factly said with all shock and sincerity, "I think God wanted you to give me your shoes."

My friend never flinched or asked another question. A few moments later, with my old, worn-out brown shoes in the wastebasket and my new brown shoes on my feet, I looked, with misty eyes, out the window as my friend walked back across the parking lot toward his little red pickup. All 6'3", bouncing dreadlocks, black leather jacket, jeans, and just socks on his feet.

It was a picture I will never forget.

A picture that pulled this big, distant, impersonal "father" out of the sky and into the very steps of my day.

Is there a God? Yes. There is a God who created and initiated the movement of life. Instead of imagining if there is a God, imagine if there wasn't. Purpose, presence, joys, sorrows, relationships, and our existence loses its immense value. God created you and me to not only exist, but to walk through life with us together.

Is God personal and present in my very life? Yes. He not only rolled out the vastness of the universe, but he also put shoes on my feet. If you process your life for a little bit, I'm confident you'll recall moments where God felt very close. Or moments that someone, in his stead, provided for you in a way that was above and beyond what you planned for or imagined. And on and on and on. God does not want you to push him to the outer reaches of your life. Instead, he wants to be in your life.

Are there miracles today? Yes. But sometimes I think we are looking for the lamp to shake or our jacket pocket to suddenly be full of money or that our loved one will instantly be cured of cancer. Sometimes those things do happen, but miracles in God's world are happening all the time. When a friend helps another friend with a difficult situation. When a spouse says he or she is sorry. When we thought we wouldn't be able to pay our bills by month's end, but somehow we did. When we anonymously gave money to a friend who found it (miraculously) in his jacket pocket.

IT'S NOT LIKE YOU PRAY FOR SHOES, AND HE GIVES YOU SHOES

I was meeting a friend for coffee. I was still reeling from how I had received my new brown shoes the day before. And they sure felt good on my feet. We were discussing the idea that God provides for our needs. Not necessarily the things we want, but the things we need. I sensed the discussion was difficult for my friend, who grew notice-ably fidgety and uncomfortable. I wasn't sure what to do. I paused and then asked, "Are you okay?"

"Yes, I'm okay. But I'm struggling to accept or grasp some of this," he replied, tears forming in his eyes.

"In what way? Did I say something wrong?"

"It's not that," he insisted. "It's just that I have the hard-est time accepting that God has any interest in me, let alone my requests. I find it hard to believe that he cares. I mean, it's not like you one day just pray for . . ." He paused, searching for an example. "It's not like you pray for shoes, and God gives you shoes!"

I jumped a bit in my seat. *Did he just say what I thought he said?* I thought. *That God doesn't give you a pair of shoes because you asked for them?* I paused and felt agitated my-self. *Should I share the story of my brown shoes from yesterday?* I asked myself. Finally, I couldn't hold it back and said, "Well, that's not entirely true . . ."

CHAPTER 4

WORMS AND GOD

It was a perfect early summer evening. Clear sky, comfortable temperature, and a gentle breeze. When you live in the north, days like this can be few and far between, so that meant one thing: burgers on the back deck with the family. We had three kids at the time, a seven-year-old boy, a four-year-old girl, and a two-year-old boy. As the kids finished their meals, they ran over to the playground area about twenty feet away and played on the swings and slide.

At those ages, it's almost as if they simply coexist near each other. They don't know yet how to play effectively together or to truly encourage one another. The only real interaction they might have is when someone else has something they want. When that happens, they stumble over, grab it, and walk away. All that does is create cascading emotions of anger and chaos.

So while they monkeyed around "near" each other, I crossed my fingers, held my breath, and shot out a prayer because Susan and I had a rare thing going here—no one needed anything and no one was crying. We leaned back, put our feet up on the table, and found a moment to enjoy conversation and a glass of wine without interruption.

That special space of time ended about five minutes later when our youngest let out an enormous scream. Not a scream of pain, but a scream of fear. Instinctively I jumped to my feet, nearly spilling my drink, and was just about to yell out, "Are you okay?" But what I saw prevented me from saying anything. I quickly realized no one was hurt and that something unique and special was unfolding. I stared, unable to move as I watched this subtle, but unforgettable moment.

The scream of fear was triggered from what had been found in the mulch while my youngest had been digging— a worm. Not just any worm, but one of those long, meaty earthworms that fishermen use for bait (or so I've heard). And, even though boys traditionally tend to like slimy things, the first encounter can be alarming for even them.

But it wasn't the worm discovery that caused me to

freeze; it was what I witnessed immediately after that discovery. As my youngest crab-walked backward as fast as he could, my two older ones drew closer; the oldest moved the closest while the middle one cautiously fell in line behind him. My seven-year-old boy bent over and picked up that squirming worm. As he held it, the other two were clearly afraid. But he read their fear, knelt down, and extended his worm-filled hand to the others, placing his free hand on his sister's shoulder to gently draw her in. "It's okay; it isn't going to hurt you," I heard him say.

This small event was the most beautiful moment I had experienced as a father. I witnessed my children shift from their selfish, mere coexistence to siblinghood. It was the first time I had seen them look at each other with sincere trust, the first time I had seen them brought together in adversity, working together, each needing the other.

In that moment, I saw them become "family." And that brought me joy. Immense joy.

As I sat back down next to Susan, I said, "You know, I don't think there is anything on the planet that brings me more joy than watching our kids interacting, getting along, and trusting one another."

That silly and seemingly forgettable event moved me. When my children connect and express love for one another, I see beauty in them.

About an hour later, we were cleaning up the dishes and I asked Susan, "Do I find more joy when our children follow our orders and obey our rules or when I see them connecting and getting along?" I knew the answer already. I received immensely more from their developing relationships than from their passion to behave. Susan thought for a moment and agreed. We discussed the satisfaction and pleasure we experience when we witness the rare moments of positive interaction between our children. It really is something that brings joy.

My children are older now (my oldest is thirteen and I have one more little girl who is five), and just last night we had our first snowstorm in nearly three months. All the kids wanted to go outside and play in it. As I ran the snow-blower back and forth on the driveway, I watched closely out of the corner of my eye as all four of them piled onto one sled and laughed and laughed as they came crashing down a small hill next to the driveway. I watched them race to the hilltop over and over, tripping each other, teasing and laughing. So much laughing.

No, it's not always like this. Rarely, in fact. But when those moments happen, when my children interact authentically, get along, laugh together, trust and love one another, I feel joy. I like it when they follow my set of rules, but it's no substitute for this feeling.

JOY AND GOD

These events have echoed deeply in my soul. Because, as I mentioned earlier, God is like a heavenly parent to us. And if I'm experiencing my children giving me joy through their interactions, it causes me to ask questions about God as our "Father" and how that reflects upon my experience as a parent and father.

It's part of being human to ask questions like, "Is there a God?" and "If he does exist, what does he want with me?" But this experience was pushing me to a new question: "What brings joy to God?"

When my wife surprises me with "taco night" at our house, that makes me happy. When I find a few spare dollars in my pocket or time to sit for my favorite movie, that also makes me happy.

But joy is different. Joy is deeper than happiness and rises from within the soul rather than from circumstance. It redefines a situation, makes it more meaningful, and you feel it in your bones.

When one of my children climbs on my lap and wants to be held, I experience joy. Or when I have a thoughtful conversation with someone who is considering a more meaningful understanding of God, that brings me joy. Or when I can spend time with Susan at our favorite restaurant, alone, just connecting. Yes, that brings me incredible joy.

Now consider God. What could he possibly want or need that would cause him to pause, take notice, and then smile? What would provoke joy in the creator's heart and make him want to shout throughout the heavens?

In the fifth chapter of Ephesians in the Bible, the writer encourages us to find what is pleasing to God (see Ephesians 5:10). In other words, try to find the things that bring joy to God.

Do we know what those things are?

When I ask people if they know what brings joy to God, the response is often immediate:

"God wants me to go to church more."
Or, "God wants me to be a good person."
Or even, "God wants me to obey that list of laws (Ten Commandments) he created."
Or finally, "God wants me to stay away from sin."

Those responses are relevant. The Bible does speak to how we live our lives and the choices we make. God does call us to a higher level of living should we choose to personally follow him. But I'm not talking about those things. I'm asking, what brings a thrill to God? What would make him say, "And that's why I created people"?

The morning after the worm experience, I thought about my earlier question to Susan and then asked myself:

Does God experience more joy when his creation, his people, follow a set of rules and ritualistic practices, or when he sees his children, his beloved and cherished creation, connecting with one another and showing love to one another? This thought shook my world. I began to ask:

When a person takes time to connect with a dear friend, does that bring joy to God?

When a person cares for a sick friend, does God experience joy there?

When a husband apologizes (sincerely) to his wife? God MUST rejoice in that.

When a mom takes a walk with her child and encourages them in their questions?

When a dad gets down on the floor and wrestles with his children?

When you call your father just to tell him you love him? Does God well up with joy?

When a broken marriage finds seeds of hope because both are willing to try again?

When a broken friendship is restored?

When a person stops the car to help another person change their tire?

When a person apologizes... period?

When a worker thanks his boss?

When a boss recognizes an employee's hard work?

When someone from one culture finds connection
with someone of another?
When a Jew and a Christian share a coffee?
When a Muslim and a Christian share a laugh?
When a Muslim and a Jew share a meal?
When a dad makes breakfast for his children?
When you stop and pick up the dropped mitten of
the person walking to the train ahead of you?

A hint is found in "creation." Genesis tells us that God
created us. He made people in his image. We are his very
image. That shapes my understanding of the intentionality
of the life I experience here. Do the very joys I experience in this life mirror the joys God feels and experiences?
Do the things I value as good and wonderful and just mirror the things he values as good and wonderful and just?
Maybe instead of asking that as a question, it would be better to make it a statement: the joys I experience here in this
life mirror the emotions and joys our heavenly father feels
and experiences because we are created in his very image.

Joy is different than the "good" one might feel in something corrupt or destructive. What "makes me feel good"
is different from knowing that something is truly good and
amazing to God. Joy is not derived from bad things, but
from things of God.

One might think that most of this means very little. But

jump back to the writer of Ephesians in the Bible. His encouragement to us is to imitate God in everything we do. We are to do so because God considers us as his dear children. And because we are God's actual children, he wants us to live our lives filled with loving others. The model for us, the writer describes, is God's own son, Jesus, because Jesus was offered as a sacrifice for us. He sacrificed his life for all of us. It is what is inherent in that kind of sacrifice, the writer says, that is the very "sweet aroma" to God (see Ephesians 5:2).

What brings joy to God? What makes the creator of the universe pause and say, "And that's why I created people"?

It is the love we share with each other and the sacrifice we make for one another. Beautiful.

Until my children found that worm, I thought love for "others" meant to love people I am not normally connected to or people I don't know yet, to love those who are less fortunate or who we serve through ministries or outreach programs, to love those difficult to love. Those are important, of course, but love for one another is substantially more profound when you consider that it really begins with the people you interact with the most.

Like the person you first see when you open your eyes in the morning.

What brings joy to God? What is a sweet aroma to him? When the spouse next to you feels your hand on their back in the morning. When you stop to listen to them when you normally shift into your gears of routine. When you make them coffee before they ask. When you help your child who cannot seem to get their backpack pulled together. When you help your next-door neighbor lift something from their car. When your coworker, the one you see every single weekday, needs help meeting their deadline and you don't have the time, but you do it anyway.

I'm a morning person. I like to get up most mornings to help Susan get our kids fed and out the door for their buses. On a recent morning my alarm sounded off at 6 a.m. It's my signal to make my way downstairs to find my thirteen-year-old son eating cereal, reading the latest sports updates on the computer, and waiting for me to get his lunch together. He can make the lunch himself, but I want to be there with him and I enjoy packing it up for him. We talk a bit, usually about hockey or football. Nothing too meaningful, and that's okay.

When it's about time for him to go out, I grab him and give him a big hug. I tell him I love him and that I will be praying for his day ahead. He cracks a half smile and says, "Thanks...love you too" just the way you imagine a thirteen-year-old boy would say it, words limping out of his mouth.

As we clean up after round one, my five-year-old daughter is usually the next one to show up, seeking hugs and food. Eventually the other two join us, and breakfast is served. Then backpacks and lunches are prepared while showers are taken and teeth are brushed and last-minute papers are signed. Susan and I drink our coffee as we finish the details and then nudge the last kids out the door to their bus.

This depiction of our mornings is misleading. Of course it is never this easy or peachy. Unexpected twists like forgotten homework, dropped milk, knotted shoes, lost coats, tears, and missed buses always find their way into this routine that connects us as a family.

Think about your morning routine now, with the lens of God watching and anticipating. His experience of joy is when he sees his creation—his children—connecting, interacting, and loving one another. The joy that ignites heaven is when I bend down to my daughter, crying because her shoestrings are in a knot, and place my hand on her cheek and tell her it is going to be okay. The love we experience and share, even in our routine, is that sweet aroma to God.

ENTRUSTED

Jesus shared a story about a man who would soon be traveling on a long journey (see Matthew 25:14–30). Before he left, Jesus said, the man called together three individuals who worked for him and told them he was going to entrust each of them with some of his money.

Not just any amount of money. A lot of money. The first worker received the equivalent of about a thousand pounds of gold. The second worker, six hundred pounds. And the third, two hundred. I would conclude that the unevenness of the allotted amounts was in proportion to how much the man trusted each of his employees. Clearly, then, the first individual was pretty special.

Being entrusted with immense value is a theme in this story. But it doesn't end there. The story also includes what these individuals do with their gold. The first employee took the enormous wealth and, through trades, he doubled his amount. The second did the same. But the third, the one who received the least, didn't do anything to grow what he had received. Instead, he buried the money until his employer returned home.

Jesus ends his story by telling us that the one who did nothing with what he had received is the one who had failed.

In your life, what do you have of immense value? Is there someone who is more valuable to you than anything else? That person or those persons are God's personal creation. Not yours. Even if you birthed the child you hold most precious, all are first God's creatures. He graciously entrusts that little child to us. Or our spouse, sibling, best friend, or parent. And because of that, the sweet aroma to God is when you invest in and love those whom he has placed around you already.

Jesus is intentional with his stories, including this one. The employer actually represents God. And just as the employer entrusted something of immense value to his staff, God has entrusted something of even greater value to you and to me. Yes, those closest to you represent the incredible wealth in the story. How you handle what has been entrusted to you—even in a morning routine—has enormous implications for how God will entrust you with other things.

Investment of time and love and energy into that which we have been entrusted is the point here, not money. In this story, Jesus is teaching us to invest in those we most treasure. Yes, we are to love others with whom we don't normally interact or those we want to reach out to, but in addition, the love we intentionally invest in the people we are most naturally close to is incredibly and undeniably valuable.

Our spouses, children, parents, siblings, neighbors, friends, baristas, mechanics, doctors, coworkers, and whomever we walk with on our unique path every day: these are the individuals entrusted to our care.

Sometimes I imagine that God asks me, "Rob, I've

entrusted into your presence some of my most valuable creations. How are they doing in your care?" I don't overwhelm those people with my time. Rather, I intentionally invest love through listening, encouraging, helping, or any other way that I can. And because I know that brings joy to God, it brings value to what I'm investing in.

I translate love and investment as the "sweet aroma" God is looking for. It's not the rules we follow, nor the desperate attempt to do everything correctly. No. It's his creation loving his creation.

It is what I believe makes God say, "And that's why I created people."

And if God describes those in our lives as his valuable creation, then what could he possibly think about you?

CHAPTER 5

THE TREASURE

How in the world could God care about me? He's God, and I'm one of billions of people. Scientifically and genetically, I know I'm unique, but I don't always feel God knows who I am or cares what I do. It's hard to imagine that God has any focus on my life. Or does he? Does God care about you and me? When you pray to him, do you feel that he's listening? Or not?

Easter morning I was driving with my ten-year-old daughter to church. "Daddy?" she said ever so gently.

"What is it, honey?" I felt the onset of a moment when a child wants to share something special with you. Something like "I love you." Or maybe more profound, like

"I've met all my friend's dads and none of them are as great as you. In fact, all my friends think you're the best dad too." But this time I had misread the tone.

"Daddy? You know what? Your hair is really turning gray." Smile.

Thanks. A lot. An innocent but felt blow to my self-image, from a ten-year-old. I thought more about what she said as I drove. I didn't mind her words too much. Maybe it makes me look more distinguished? My feelings about my hair are intertwined with my overall "self-image." Most of us care at least what some people think about us. It matters to us how we look or what our house looks like when someone comes to visit. We care about our weight and our clothes and our car and even the whiteness of our teeth. Even if we don't want to be concerned about our image, it's hard not to.

Sometimes people care about image in a way that makes them want to be noticed; they might buy expensive, bright, or noticeable clothes. Others care in a way that leads them to blend in, not to draw attention—that person who wears khaki everything. On rare occasions you might meet someone who doesn't care what almost anyone thinks, like the dad who wore a T-shirt to my son's school musical that said, "Do I look like a people person?" in huge letters on the back. I don't think he cares what most people think. And no, he didn't look like a people person.

But deep down, he probably cares very much what a few people in his life think of him. Most of us do care about our image. We care what people think.

HUMBLE BEGINNINGS

When I was in high school, my dad helped me purchase and fix up my first car—a 1981, two-door hatchback, navy-blue Plymouth TC3 (a close cousin of the also for- gotten Dodge O24). Not as bad as a Gremlin, it was my first car, and living in Minnesota in the distant suburbs of Minneapolis, this car was fine. In fact, I grew quite fond of the little thing.

Until I crashed it nine months later on an icy road in the dead of winter in a head-on collision. A head-on with a school bus, that is. Yes, a huge, can't-miss-it, yel- low school bus. And while the school bus, the kids on the bus, and I myself didn't suffer a single scratch (I hit the front tire of the bus), my car was not so fortunate. It was nearly totaled and would require significant rebuilding to ever run again.

When the dust had settled and I was safe at home, I real- ized my crushed blue babe was a picture of my humiliation. Word threaded its way through the student body that I had hit a school bus. That's just not cool. That's low-hanging fruit, even for those who don't customarily tease. I quickly realized I now had an image problem.

A few months later, my dad and I worked to resurrect my car from parts we purchased off of junked cars at local salvage yards. Bit by bit, we rebuilt and patched it back together with all kinds of new parts in interesting colors. I was proud of that work. But as I drove it around town, it was an unmistakable and unforgettable collage of vehicular humiliation.

In the shadow of that humiliation, one desperate day I tried to match the multicolored area of the car with a blue spray can of car paint I found at a local auto parts store. But that only created a whole new and odd-looking shade of blue. It was now a two-toned blue-colored car. I thought maybe the two tones were fine until the first day I rolled onto my college campus near Chicago. I felt like Mater from the *Cars* movie, as beautiful Mercedes and BMWs and Land Rovers rolled past me, winking, pointing, and giggling.

So when I asked Susan to go out with me for our first date, I thought long and hard about borrowing a friend's car to take her out rather than driving my sad machine. I was concerned about my image and I didn't want an old, beat-up car to determine what she thought of me.

I asked my roommate and two other friends if their cars were free, but to no avail. With time running out, I conceded and accepted that I would be driving mine. As we drove through the streets of Chicago, I hung my head even lower when one end of my muffler suddenly crashed to the street, scaring both of us. It must have rotted through. We weren't in a place where I could pull over, and as I drove on, the incredibly loud, dragging muffler shot sparks from underneath my car. Pedestrians pointed and laughed. I finally found a place to park and I desperately prayed as I opened the hatchback and felt around in the dark for a bungee cord. Note: always carry a bungee cord in an old car. Thank you, God. I found one. After some time on my back, under my car, on the wet pavement, I was able to hoist the muffler temporarily into place. As I lay there, I paused and thought about Susan sitting inside the car. What must she be thinking right now? The grease on my face and the humiliation in my heart, I believe, led Susan to take pity on me and give me another chance. I had im-age problems.

We all do things to try to look good or create a certain image. Or we take enormous steps to prevent a bad image. And if we have a good image, we work hard to maintain it. We want to be seen in a certain light. We want people to like us based on an image we intentionally create. That's normal. Not always good for us, but normal. This desire for a good image is connected to our need for two things: acceptance and approval.

Acceptance

We want people to accept us, not ignore us. We want to be a part of a group. It requires time and energy to look or act a certain way so that we can be accepted. The door to acceptance in our culture is directly linked to our appearance. So it makes sense that we are so intentional in our purchases of clothes, shoes, hair products, deodorants, razors, dyes, clippers, hair trimmers and blowers, glasses, contacts, makeup, perfumes, pushup bras, rings, earrings, necklaces, purses, bags, tights, and whatever else we can get on our bodies after we've run, jumped, stretched, yoga'd, lifted, and lapped because of our calorie or carb count. Our "investment" in these things is to create an image or to avoid a bad one. The pressure to bring all of these items and accessories into a harmonious presentation that makes us acceptable to others is overwhelming.

Acceptance is also a driving force behind why we strive to accomplish things. It's the driving force behind grades, evaluations, proposals, and sport records, for example. When we build a home, close a deal, get a job, sign a contract, or when we attempt to create something unique, we are seeking assurance that we are accepted. All of these things, while often good, influence our understanding of being "acceptable" in our society. Acceptance is about fitting in and not being left out. It often means we work and strive to do well enough or dress well enough so that we aren't singled out and left behind.

Approval

We also want approval from others. Although similar to acceptance, approval is still unique because it's what drives us to receive a nod or smile from someone else, sometimes at the expense of being ourselves. Do I do things for others in order to attain their approval? It's a tough question to face and answer honestly. If I'm consistently seeking approval from others, I will ultimately become a shadow of who I really am. I lose myself when I seek approval from others because I become someone who pleases a certain percentage of the people I am connected to, and then I try to become someone else to another percentage. Pretty soon, and I've experienced this personally, I'm not really myself. Instead I've become someone others feel I should be. That's exhausting. And frustrating. And never, ever works.

The pursuits of acceptance and approval fuel our desire to have a good "image." That fuel burns deep within us, and if it isn't managed, it can drive us to do ridiculous things, like desperately spray-painting a car without really checking to see if the color matched.

I've thought a lot about the way our need for acceptance

and approval presses so heavily on our lives. Several years ago I decided to turn the question toward Jesus. And it followed this kind of thinking: How does Jesus see me? When he looks upon me, what does he think? And then, if I knew how Jesus saw me, would it impact how I see myself? Would it impact my need or desire to be accepted? Would it affect or even change how I think or feel about myself and my "image"?

A NEW PICTURE

It would be significant if Jesus' impression of us reshaped how we viewed our own self-images.

The Bible talks about image and our desire to look good in the eyes of others in a number of places. However, there is one little verse, one little gem, that brings this home in a visceral and cerebral way for me. This one little verse altered how I think about and process my own image of myself.

It is found right in the middle of one of my favorite parts of the Bible, in the thirteenth chapter of Matthew. In this chapter Jesus tells a series of fictional stories designed to reveal a greater purpose. The "parables" in this chapter all depict what the Kingdom of Heaven, otherwise known as the Kingdom of God, is like. (It is accepted in Christianity that the Kingdom of Heaven and the Kingdom of God are interchangeable. For this chapter, I'll use the phrase Kingdom of God.) It's as if Jesus is filling a photo album for you to visualize a special reality he's revealing.

This Kingdom he describes is not a monarchy led by a king. And that's important to note because that would be precisely what the people of Jesus' day would be looking for—a new, "king-led" monarchy that would rid their land of the Romans who currently governed over them in their own territory. The Kingdom, then, was a very significant subject, even in the stories and parables that Jesus told.

But Jesus was describing a "Kingdom of God" that was entirely different than what his listeners would have imagined. He was articulating that God's Kingdom was a place where divine intentions not only unfold before our eyes, but are actually brought into our reality through those of us who are followers of Jesus. This "Kingdom" is actually something all of us are a part of.

In order to see the enormous confusion and tension that Jesus' teachings created in the thirteenth chapter of the book of Matthew, we look at a very revealing exchange between Jesus and the religious leaders. It is found in the book of Luke 17:20–21.

"When will the Kingdom of God come?" the religious leaders asked.

This question is loaded. It was designed to confound Jesus and put him in a corner. If Jesus answered that question with an actual date, the religious leaders would assume that would be the time when he and his ragtag followers would mount up an army and face off against the Romans, bringing about a new Kingdom for Israel. Who was this man, Jesus, to insinuate that he could do such a thing?

But Jesus wasn't trapped. In fact, he had an entirely different image of what the Kingdom looked like:

> The Kingdom of God isn't ushered in with visible signs (or speculations). You won't be able to say, "Here it is!" or "It's over there!" For the Kingdom of God is among/ within you.

His answer was striking. Jesus wasn't falling prey to the implications they were making about a military insurrection. Rather, he was describing something that resided in the here and now. The Kingdom, he said, isn't something tangible like a building or a tower or a castle, but rather, it is something that emerges from our very core, inside of us. The Kingdom is something we participate in. Even if we are in incredibly difficult situations, God's Kingdom resides in us and comes from us to touch the world around us.

So imagine the shock the religious leaders felt when Jesus described the Kingdom not as a place one builds and establishes physically, but instead as something that already exists within and among us.

Imagine my shock when I first studied this passage. The leaders expected a literal earthly kingdom. I, however, had an entirely different image of the Kingdom in my own head. I pictured it as a blissful place with God, beyond here. I was imagining that when Jesus described the Kingdom, he was describing heaven after we die. But Jesus is talking about a Kingdom that already exists here and now. And it is brought into our presence through you and me.

To see this on an entirely new level, look at what Jesus says to another religious leader, Nicodemus, who sneaks through the evening darkness to meet secretly with Jesus (see John 3). In public settings, religious leaders often challenged Jesus, and private consultations with him were considered unacceptable. So when this cloaked, nervous Jewish leader sat privately with Jesus, he was taking a risk with his life. But he quietly believed in Jesus. And he immediately complimented him by saying that he acknowledged that God was clearly with Jesus. Again Jesus responded in a most interesting way:

Unless you've been born anew/again, you cannot [ever] see the Kingdom of God.

John 3:3 [added for emphasis]

Did you catch that? Unless you're born anew with Jesus, you will not be able to "SEE" the Kingdom.

Considering what he said to the religious leaders about the Kingdom being in our very presence, what is Jesus really saying? I propose it is something like this: "Nicodemus, the simple reality is that unless you are surrendered to God and open to accepting me (being born anew), the most incredible Kingdom will be present all around you and you'll never even see it. In fact, you'll miss it entirely."

We tease my oldest son that he's not the most observant person around. "Hey, would you grab those chairs for the sidelines when you make your way to the car?" I stood in the driveway watching him as he tied his soccer cleats on the steps inside the garage. I had laid two foldable chairs twelve inches from his feet as I made my way out to the car. I needed a little help and hoped he'd pitch in by grabbing the chairs.

When he was done, I watched from a distance as he stood up, scanned the nearly empty garage, and then turned around 180 degrees and looked at the door going into the house.

"Dad, I don't see those chairs anywhere."

"They're right by your feet," I said, starting to laugh to myself.

"What? Where?"

72

"Turn around, carefully. You'll trip on them if you turn too quickly."

Right in front of him, but completely unable to see them.

Jesus' description of the Kingdom of God to Nicodemus is similarly overt. Unless you pursue God, the Kingdom of God can be shooting fireworks right in front of you and you'll never ever see it.

THE LITTLE, TINY, ITTY-BITTY VERSE THAT CHANGES EVERYTHING

So, as I mentioned earlier, when we return to the little verse found in Matthew 13, along with the other stories and parables that describe the Kingdom of God, we know that Jesus isn't describing a huge castle on a hill with peasants catering to the king's every need. Nor is he describing what heaven might look like someday when we die. Rather, he is unveiling a Kingdom from God that flows in our midst through the people who follow him. Whether in the United States, Kenya, China, Iran, Brazil, Iceland, or anywhere else, the Kingdom of God is revealing itself through those who are born anew.

These parables are meaningful for you and me. Crucial. Jesus describes what this Kingdom of God is like through the Matthew 13 series of parables, almost the same way one might pull out their phone and slide through their pictures from a recent trip to Disney World with a friend who's never been there. The parables are glimpses of the bigger picture. When pieced together, one gets a very interesting image of this Kingdom.

The Treasure

But, as I said earlier, in this series of parables about the Kingdom in Matthew 13, there is one particular tiny verse, just two short sentences, that carries significant meaning about our image of ourselves. It's found in Matthew 13:44, and these are Jesus' words (NLT):

> The Kingdom of God is like a treasure that a man discovered hidden in a field. In his excitement, he hid it again and sold everything he owned to get enough money to buy the field.

In parables, the main characters intentionally carry important and loaded meanings. In this parable there are three main characters: the treasure, the man, and the field. On first glance, it appears obvious who these characters represent. The treasure would seem to represent the Kingdom of God. "The Kingdom is like a treasure..." the verse says clearly.

The man, then, seems to represent you and me or all of us in the world—humankind.

Finally, the field seems to represent culture or the world or the present life we live.

Character	Meaning
The Man	You and Me
The Field	Our World/Culture
The Treasure	The Kingdom of God

When we revisit this verse and add the meaning of the identified characters, it would read something like this:

> The Kingdom of God is a treasure. A man (you or me) was walking through a field (through life) and upon that discovery, he reburied the treasure. He (you or me) then went and sold everything he owned in order to attain the treasure (the Kingdom).

One could conclude from this verse that the Kingdom of God is so valuable and wonderful that it is worth giving up every single thing I have—my house, my car, my job, my relationships, or anything I own—in order to attain it. It looks like Jesus is teaching that the Kingdom of God is so precious that I should be willing to do anything or give up everything so I can then get it.

And the Kingdom of God is so important that I don't let the things of this world distract me from it. It is the most significant thing I can imagine.

Upon further review, however, that interpretation doesn't feel right to me. Something is wrong.

That's frustrating because nearly every book I've ever read about this verse presents a meaning very similar to what I've just presented. But I just know something is deeply flawed about that approach.

It took me a while, but eventually it hit me. And it was triggered from something I read years ago by Robert Farrar Capon, an elderly Episcopal priest on Long Island, New York. He has written many books. In one on parables, he makes the case that nearly all of Jesus' parables include a character in the story who represents God.

A God-character in each of the parables? Yes. And what is missing in our little chart? Yes, a God-character. Nothing in our chart represents God or Jesus...the treasure, the field, the man. None of them met the criteria. And that creates a problem because we might just be missing an enormous and powerful discovery.

So, in revisiting this little, tiny verse, it looks like this:

"The Kingdom of God is like a treasure that a man discovered hidden in a field. In his excitement, he hid it again and sold everything he owned to get enough money to buy the field."

Is the treasure our God-character? Is it the field? The man?

Here is how I break it down. The field is still the same: it represents our culture and our world. The treasure doesn't fit, and I need to come back to that later. Which leaves the man. Yes, the man does not represent you and me. But instead, it is actually Jesus (our God-character). Look at the story again with Jesus as the man:

"The Kingdom of God is like a treasure (?) that a man (Jesus) found hidden in a field (the world). In his (Jesus') excitement he sold everything he owned in order to get enough money to buy the field so he could get the treasure."

The new chart now looks like this, so far:

Character	Meaning
The Man	Jesus
The Field	Our World/Culture
Treasure	?

What, then, does the treasure represent? The treasure is NOT the Kingdom of God because Jesus isn't describing the Kingdom of God as something that he discovered. That wouldn't work. If he is the one who ushers in the Kingdom, then he wouldn't "stumble" upon it. In addition, to describe the Kingdom of God as a valuable treasure wouldn't work with Jesus' style of teaching because when he taught, he shocked his listeners. He challenged everything they ever believed and flipped it upside down. His listeners, especially the religious leaders, would not have been shocked at all by our initial translation of the Kingdom of God being as valuable as a treasure. The audience would have actually agreed with that notion. So much so that someone might have yelled "Amen!" from the back. No, this verse is far, far more potent than that. It is also far more provocative. Jesus is proposing something new to this audience. Something that they not only had never heard of, but also something they couldn't fully wrap their minds around until a later date.

If the man in the story is Jesus walking through the field (our world and our culture), and he discovers a treasure, then what in the world is the treasure? What valuable thing could he possibly find? If it's not the Kingdom of God, then what is it?

The treasure ...

is none other than ...

you.

Character	Meaning
The Man	Jesus
The Field	Our World/Culture
The Treasure	You

You Are the Treasure

The implications of this teaching in this little, tiny verse are huge, and they directly affect you and me. They especially affect our self-image. Jesus is speaking into the future here—specifically, teaching a concept of inevitability. Through the verse he is revealing to his listeners, the crowd...

> I (Jesus) was walking through a field and discovered a treasure (You). I then gave up everything I have...everything...for this treasure (You). I am even willing to give up my own life for it (You).

Jesus sees you as so incredibly valuable. So valuable, in fact, that he was willing to surrender his life for yours. Even when you're one of billions, he died for you. He sees each of us as uniquely valuable.

Where do you find that kind of love? Acceptance? Approval?

While we are endlessly engaged in improving and bettering our self-image, we are hiding who we are, compromising, changing, adjusting, and working on every part of ourselves so that we will be accepted and approved by others, people who are doing the exact same thing to themselves for you and others.

What if you were already incredibly valuable? What if Jesus sees you as so valuable that you are a treasure to him? And he proved that by dying for you? What would happen if you knew that you were already, without all the changes and improvements, valuable enough that someone would love you? You know that feeling you get when you receive a nod of affirmation from a loved one. It is so empowering for that moment. So encouraging. It doesn't last, but it helps get you through difficult times. But Jesus unconditionally loves you in such a profound way that he told this parable about you—he was telling those listening then and today that he was going to discover you, his treasure, and give up everything for you.

For me, embracing that I am the treasure Jesus found frees me from seeking acceptance and approval in the world. It is the birth of being okay with me. It is the beginning of knowing I'm already accepted and already approved. I'm not perfect, but I am far more at ease in life with this knowledge.

Jesus reveals one more incredibly profound aspect of the Kingdom of God. The Kingdom is not a treasure. That is,

it is not a static pile of pretty metal. There is another way
to see it:

> Do you want to know what the Kingdom of God is like?
> It is *like a man (Jesus) who finds a treasure (You) hidden in a
> field (the World)*.

The Kingdom of God isn't a precious metal but the active,
constantly moving, incredible process of Jesus finding you,
and others.

That is the Kingdom of God—Jesus finding people . . .
forever.

It never stops. He is always connecting and reconnecting with us. The Kingdom of God is the ongoing,
relationship-building, love-giving act of Jesus finding you
and giving up his life for you.

As I drove to church that Easter morning, realizing I'm
getting older and grayer, I glanced at my daughter while she
silently gazed out the side window. Time froze for just a brief
moment. I held my breath. But my heart for her was a steady
beat in the stillness. Ten years old. Innocent. Precious. At that
moment my daughter was my treasure. I would die for her—
that is how much I value her. And in that moment I knew
Jesus died for her and for me because we are that valuable to
him. We are his treasure. When you realize you're someone's
treasure, it empowers you. It changes you. It frees you.

CHAPTER 6

IF ONLY YOU HAD BEEN HERE

I remember exactly where I was on February 22, 1980. I was in my living room, running and jumping while watching the United States Olympic Hockey Team on TV play the final minutes of their "Miracle on Ice" game against the Soviet Union. I couldn't sit still. I moved all about the living room with a hockey stick in my hand. I watched with feelings of fear, excitement, and, especially, hope.

Hope.

Before the game there was almost no hope. Even after the second period there was little hope. The conclusion was already scripted. The Soviets were expected to win. However, as the game rolled along, hope spread like wildfire across our nation, even to a nine-year-old boy in his Minnesota home. *This could happen*, I thought.

Hope.

Hope is that encouraging and powerful feeling that what is wanted can be had or that events will turn out okay or for the best. It is uplifting to experience hope at a climactic level like the Olympic games. But I've come to realize over the years that supermoments aren't the only place I experience it. I experience hope in many less dramatic or even subtle ways. For instance, I hope people around me will do the right thing. I hope my children have good teachers who will do their best in educating them. I hope the law will protect my family and me. I hope my investments will give me good returns. I hope my favorite TV show won't be a repeat this week. I even hope the sun will come out today. Hope keeps me moving.

Hope keeps us all moving. Most of us have glimmers of hope in very basic things. Without hope, trudging through life is incredibly difficult. It is why we pull ourselves out of bed in the morning. Interestingly many of us share three significant, but almost imperceptible, "hopes." We don't even acknowledge these specific hopes most of the time, but they are still present and important to us.

HOPE: LIFE HERE AND NOW

The first hope is assumed and is often taken for granted. It is all around us, and it deals with our life today, right here, right now.

Each evening we lay our heads down and trust or hope that we will arise the next morning. We wake up and have hope about our day ahead. We don't set out to cease to exist. We plan to be here and to progress.

Recently I was driving home from work, and while waiting at a stoplight for the left-turn signal, a blaring and lit-up police car and a similarly urgent ambulance raced through the intersection. A police car alone most likely reveals that someone did something wrong. An ambulance alone tells me someone is probably hurt or suffering in their home. A police car and an ambulance together—and then a fire truck that blazed by—told the whole story. There was, most likely, a vehicle accident nearby.

My assumptions were correct. After the emergency vehicles roared by, I took my left, in the same direction they were headed. I made my way only about a half mile before I noticed black smoke shooting out of the dense trees along the road and into the sky ahead. As I cautiously drew closer to the accident scene, I saw fire and the safety workers jumping out of their vehicles to attend to an obviously horrific scene. This accident had happened just minutes before.

Both lanes of the road were blocked with the emergency vehicles, and people stood outside their cars on this small two-lane town road near the local elementary school. And then I saw the man. He lay motionless in the street. His motorcycle was fifty yards beyond him, on fire, leaning against a wildly burning wooden telephone pole.

As I watched the team trying to save him, the man appeared to be straddling the fine line between life and death. Five minutes earlier, this man on the motorcycle was not thinking life might escape him around the next corner. He didn't know that a van, driven by a seventeen-year-old new driver, would hit him head-on.

Life. Although we take it for granted, we hope it will continue. We hope we will see our loved ones indefinitely. I have hope when I'm done writing today that I will drive home and see my children. This life, on this earth, is filled with a sense of hope that we will experience life itself as an ongoing reality. It's our hope in the "here and now."

HOPE: BEYOND NOW

The second hope is real and personal to many of us, yet we rarely talk about it because we don't know how much we can put into it. We have the strongest sense of hope for it when we gather at the funeral of a loved one. This second hope many of us hold is that there is a life after this one, a place beyond here. Some call it heaven. And although we almost never openly talk about it with our coworkers or neighbors, most of us hope deep down that when our loved ones die, we will see them again.

I remember hearing our doorbell ring over and over at 6:30 a.m. in my childhood home when I was eleven. Who could be so eager to ring the doorbell at that hour? I have always been a light sleeper, so when I raised my head from my pillow, I knew I'd be the one to answer. I also remembered that my fourteen-year-old sister wasn't home; she'd spent the night at a friend's house. Yes, it would be me. I was old enough.

I left my room and turned left to make my way down the long hall, heading in the direction of the front door. I noticed that my parents' door was closed as I passed by. That also confirmed I would be the one.

At the end of the hall, I took another left and walked straight to the front door. I saw through the window that it wasn't a stranger ringing the doorbell; it was our next-door neighbors. Both husband and wife stood there, looking frantic and stressed. She in her nursing uniform. He in his highway patrolman uniform. Me in my pajamas and robe, my sleep uniform.

"Hi, Robbie. Can we speak to your mom and dad, please?" Mr. Frank sounded firm, but gentle. His wife seemed to be wiping away tears.

"Sure, please step in," I responded ever so politely. "I'll go get them."

I turned around, walked five paces, turned right, and headed back down the hallway toward the bedrooms. I knocked at my parents' door and told them that our neighbors were here to see them. There was a scruffled, "Okay," from the other side.

As I turned toward my bedroom, I noticed out of the corner of my eye that our neighbors were no longer at the front door but were now at the very end of our long hall.

Odd, I thought. I trusted them though. They had been great neighbors for years. Our families were pretty close, and all the kids got along.

As I took my first step into my room, I heard my parents' door open. I paused. I was now awake enough to be curious about what was going on.

And then I heard the scream. "No! No!! Not my baby girl! No!!"

I looked down the hall from my room and saw my mom running toward my neighbors, my father right behind her. I don't know how she knew, but a mom knows. She fell into my neighbors' waiting arms. Through their own shaky and emotional voices, they told her and my dad that just a few hours before, he, as a highway patrolman, had identified my sister and her friend, who had been struck by a hit-and-run car the night before. A trucker apparently saw some shoes and mittens along the road in the middle of the night. He stopped his truck, got out of the cab, and walked back to find two teenage girls facedown, dead, in a snow-filled ditch along the road.

Nothing can prepare you for that. We were devastated. My mom was broken most of all.

But intermingled with the loss and pain and injustice, even in the midst of that chaos, something pulled us through—hope that she was not gone from us forever.

(They eventually caught the driver. Witnesses at the bar earlier that night said he was drunk, but because he had disappeared from the scene that night and left the girls to die in the freezing ditch, there was no way to prove it. The next day, he told people he had hit a deer the night before and washed the blood from his car. He even attended my sister's funeral two days later because, as her competitive swim coach, he played the part of being concerned and offering condolences. A few days later, when he thought he was in the clear, the police solved the mystery and he confessed.)

We believed Lisa was with God, and that we will see her again. I truly believe that to this day. That hope helped restore us to a new normal in life.

I conduct funerals and memorial services from time to time, and I've discovered something over the years: it doesn't matter what people say to me about heaven and God before their loved one dies because at the funeral, everything changes. The day Dad or Mom or Grandpa or spouse or child in a casket is rolled into the church or funeral home, even the toughest and most defiant person is broken.

Then they yield to hope. Hope that death isn't it. Hope that there is a life beyond here. Our culture talks a good game, but when we stare death in the face, most of us choose hope rather than nothing. I see it all the time.

Consider the idea of hope in an afterlife from a religious context. Those who believe in the Judeo-Christian God believe there is a life after this current life. Those who claim any god generally have a similar belief. Some call it the afterlife. Some call it heaven. Jews call it the "Resurrection Day." Others refer to it as "up there" as they point to the white billowy clouds.

All represent the hope of something beyond here and now, the hope that we will see our loved ones someday.

The Bible is filled with descriptions and expectations of that place beyond here. You hear it in phrases like, "The LORD is God in heaven above and on the earth below" (Deuteronomy 4:39) and "God looks down from heaven on all mankind to see if there are any who understand, any who seek God" (Psalm 53:2). Christians and Jews (nearly half of the world) hope in our life here, in our present existence, and also in a life that exists beyond our world, beyond our understanding, beyond our life here. In fact, most people in our world today hope in the life after, not only religious folk.

And that leads us to our more obscure third hope, one most of us share. It is a bit unusual and, from years of observation, my term for it is that it's all about "The One."

HOPE: THE ONE

This last hope is a bit unorthodox. You may not believe we hope for what I'm about to propose, but be patient with me and see if it isn't something that resonates with you. It drives many of us to spend our time and hard-earned dollars at a movie theater. It is a storyline we connect to and never seem to tire of.

We hold out hope for "The One."

For example, we hold out hope that when aliens start obliterating our cities, "the one" will save the day. We held out hope that the kid we loved to hate (Johnny) in the original *Karate Kid* movie would meet up with "the one" (Ralph Macchio) so he could get what was coming to him. We hoped that Mark Hamill, as Luke Skywalker, would discover that he was "the one."

That Angelina Jolie would discover that she was "the one" as Lara Croft.

That Daniel Radcliffe would discover that he was "the one" as Harry Potter.

That Tobey Maguire would discover that he was "the one" as Spider-Man.

That Bruce Willis would discover that he was "the one" to save the day in *Die Hard*.

That Sigourney Weaver would discover that she was "the one" they all desperately needed in *Aliens*.

That Keanu Reeves would definitely discover that he was "the chosen one" in *The Matrix*.

And then there's Harrison Ford as Indiana Jones, Shia LaBeouf in *Transformers*, and on and on and on and on. For some reason, the phrase, "You're the one" never grows old in our culture.

I wonder if deep down in the very core of who we are, we secretly hope we might be "the one." We can't fly or stop bullets or ride-over-a-cliff-but-still-hold-on-to-the-only-remaining-branch or walk on walls, but we climb corporate ladders and try to be "the one" in the business world or the school we attend or our children attend or college world or the dance world or the sports world or the cooking world or the ministry world or the teaching world or the photography world or the blogging world or even the parenting world. In our culture, we either root for "the one" or we want to be "the one," or both.

I'm not saying it's bad. "The one" is usually the underdog, and the improbable victor is the one we root for. (Think *Hoosiers*, *Rudy*, *October Sky*, *Erin Brockovich*, *The Bad News Bears*, *We Are Marshall*, *The Blind Side*, *The Princess Diaries*, *The Mighty Ducks*, *Rambo*, *I Am Legend*, *Commando*, and even *Caddyshack*.) We love that story. It stands to reason that because we like that storyline so much, we like to think that we're "the one" in our own world.

I've thought a lot about these three specific hopes: life here, life after, and "the one" and how they are not often spoken out loud, but are ever-present in so many of us. Then I encountered an incredibly compelling story of Jesus that reveals all three and in a way we may not have ever imagined.

JESUS: THE NOW, THE THEN, THE ONE

It all started one day when Jesus and his disciples were quietly hanging out and someone stopped in, possibly out of breath from running, to share some urgent news. Apparently a dear friend of Jesus' had become quite ill and was in his last moments of life.

Jesus wasn't too near where his friend lived. But neither

was he too far away. Most likely he was on the other side of the river, several miles away. Enough distance that the trek to his friend would take some time. Close enough that he could be there probably within a day.

The proximity is important because it plays directly into the story. Upon hearing this news that his friend was very sick, Jesus did a most peculiar thing.

He did nothing.

That's right, he simply stayed where he was for several more days.

Keep in mind that by this time Jesus was well known in the region for his ability to heal people. Those closest to him had frequently witnessed amazing things and knew of his enormous earthly powers that seemed to transcend understanding. There were stories not only about him healing people, but feeding thousands with very little food, calming raging storms, and turning cisterns of water into fine wine. He had the goods, everyone would agree, to handle the healing of his dear friend. So it is interesting, then, that Jesus deliberately chose not to rush to help his friend. He chose to wait long enough to allow his friend to die. In addition, when Jesus finally did arrive, he not only encountered grieving friends and family, but discovered his friend had been dead and was decomposing in a grave for four days now.

This just doesn't make sense, does it? Why would Jesus

not show up before Lazarus died? If Jesus had the power to heal, and he was known for having that power, why would he not hurry over to help his dear friend? Why would he not race to his bedside before it was too late?

Unless, of course, he knew exactly what he was doing.

Family present at the scene, especially the dead man's sisters, had similar questions. It prompted both of them to look at Jesus and say, "If only you had been here, our brother would not have died" (see John 11:21). I imagine these mourning women don't just say these words, but instead were probably crying and screaming them at him. Others at the scene mumbled to one another about their frustration with Jesus too. They knew he had the power to heal the dead man. But they believed he had his priorities out of whack.

Have you ever gathered with some friends only to have them look at you and say, "Oh man, last night was unbelievable. If only you had been there!" You feel like you missed out on something. Something amazing. Something important. Something you can't replay or go back to. Something you just know you should have been there for. We've all felt that pang of regret. It is rare that we decide to pass up what we think is the big event.

Years ago when my grandmother died, my mother called, in tears, telling me that it had finally happened, after years of slow deterioration. I asked about the funeral details and then immediately began planning for the next day when Susan and I would need to travel to the funeral. We lived in Connecticut at the time, just outside of New York City, and needed to fly from JFK in New York City to Minneapolis the following evening to ensure that we made it to the funeral by the next afternoon. My grandmother's small hometown was a five-hour drive north of Minneapolis.

Susan and I made flight arrangements for the next evening on a small airline specifically designed to run between New York City and Minneapolis. That morning, however, we awoke to the news of a northeast hurricane in our area. We quickly packed ourselves into our car and began driving to the airport. As we drove, we faced quickly increasing bad weather. The hurricane was in full force, and the windshield wipers couldn't move fast enough. As we drove we encountered not one, not two, but three traffic entanglements. All three were caused by stalled cars that had quit after running through overwhelming water and puddles on the highway into the city. This storm was bad. The harder the rain fell, the more stress set in. I began to feel concerned that if it kept up, we might not make our flight. That wasn't setting well with me. It meant everything to my mom that I get home for this funeral. The fact that these unexpected delays were happening caused my heart to race and my fingers to squeeze the steering wheel with all my strength.

Since this event happened before we owned cell phones, we were at the mercy of the periodic radio news updates to get the latest details on the weather. Finally, while sitting in the third traffic mess, we heard that delays were everywhere, including the airports. We breathed a sigh of relief. It looked like we were going to be okay, despite the slow going.

We reached the long-term airport parking area, which was nowhere near the airport, and faced a new problem. In the distance, through the pouring rain, we could barely see the airport bus. We grabbed our bags as fast as we could and ran through the many puddles to reach it. We were just a row of cars away, but the bus must not have seen us because it pulled away completely oblivious to our screams. There we stood at the bus stop, wet and dripping. I looked around; it was only us. No one else. And it was getting darker.

"The buses come all the time," I assured Susan. "We'll be fine. We'll make the flight." I looked around to see if John Candy or Steve Martin were nearby. We were having our own *Planes, Trains, and Automobiles* scene right then. I grew discouraged, and my anxiety continued as the next bus didn't come for almost thirty minutes. Thirty minutes? At an airport parking lot in New York City? Crazy.

When we finally jumped on the next bus, I asked the

driver about the flight delays. "Everything is delayed, don't worry," he said. We felt a bit better. Wet, but better.

As we walked up to the vacant counters, I began to worry again. We knocked on doors, yelled, and finally a woman appeared through a hidden door that I couldn't see before she opened it. We handed her our tickets and said we desperately needed to get on our plane to make it for a funeral.

"Oh, I'm sorry," she said. "You're too late."

I immediately panicked. "What do you mean? Are you saying our flight is gone? And in this weather?"

"Well, the doors are closed and it's going to depart in the next few minutes," she said just too matter-of-factly for how I was feeling inside.

I looked at her, confused. "But aren't you delaying your flight? The hurricane? We heard every airline was delayed because of the hurricane. Are you saying our flight is heading out on time?" The urgency and frustration I felt was hard to hold back.

Then she said these exact words, "Oh, XYZ Airlines [name withheld] never, ever delays their planes."

Yes, she actually said that. I've flown this airline two subsequent times, by the way, and all my connecting flights were delayed. Every single one.

"Is there any way you could simply ask them to take us on?" I was begging now. "My grandmother's funeral is tomorrow."

"Sorry, we just can't do it, and it's the last flight out to Minneapolis."

I did some fruitless calling to other airlines, and even if we left in the morning early, we couldn't make the funeral. We were stuck. Helpless. Wet. And pitiful. I wasn't going to get back to help my mom through this. Oh man, the realization hit me with full force.

And I can only tell you to imagine the phone call to my mom that evening. "Mom..."

"Oh, honey, are you already in Minnesota?"

"Mom...we missed our flight. We can't make it to Grandma's funeral. I am so sorry."

Silence. Then tears. She just dropped the phone in my dad's lap.

There are times when you just should be where you were supposed to be and you blow it. It feels wrong. It eats you up. It makes you almost irrational. *We put a man on the moon!* I yelled inside my head. *And you're telling me you can't get me home to this funeral?* I wanted to control this situation, but I couldn't.

What if the situation was similar, but I intentionally didn't make the effort to show up? What if I said, "Hey Mom, I'm not coming because I don't feel the urgency to be there"? Could I be more callous?

What Jesus did by not showing up while his friend was deathly sick looked more callous than accidental. At least that's what it looks like at first glance. He chose not to rush to heal his dear friend. The tension here, however, is that everyone knew he could save him if he wanted to. To steal the words of the sisters, "If you had been here, our brother would not have died" (see John 11:21). And I'll add these words: "But it's too late now." They didn't verbally speak that last sentence, but it's implied in the emotions and feelings expressed by both sisters' reactions to Jesus' late arrival. You can almost hear it in the words of others as they say he's supposed to have power, but now it's too late.

I've wondered a lot about Jesus' actions in this story. In fact, I was even troubled when I first started reading through it. *Why wouldn't Jesus help his friend?* I thought. But then, as the rest of the story unfolded, I began to realize that Jesus had a very intentional reason for not arriving before his friend's death. In fact, I would propose that Jesus was so intentional that, ultimately, he wanted to make one of the most profound points he ever made about himself. He gave an enormous hint in this simple dialogue with Martha (see John 11:23–24):

"You know, your brother will rise again," Jesus said.

"Yes," she replied, "when everyone else eventually rises on resurrection day."

This exchange is incredibly revealing and foreshadowing.

Jesus tells this sister that her brother will rise. But her

response communicates that she doesn't understand what Jesus is really saying. Her understanding of "rise again" and "resurrection" is rooted in the historical Jewish traditions of their holy Scriptures. It is in the future. It is heaven. It is where we go when we die. It is beyond here and beyond now.

In complete contrast, however, Jesus is talking about his friend rising from the dead—now. He's saying that he will live again with all of them...right now.

Most importantly, even though the friend and brother had tried to hold on to his life, he was now gone. He had risen or moved to a place beyond this world. Forever. The sister understood that although Jesus was good and powerful, it was abundantly clear that her brother was dead. And that meant he was now beyond everyone's reach because once someone goes to the afterlife, there is a natural and clear boundary one cannot cross. They knew that the dead were out of the reach of everyone here on this earth, including Jesus.

"If you had been here..." You can hear it in the cry, can't you? "If only you had been here. If only. If only! But now...it's too late."

This makes for a movie-like situation. On the one hand, you have Jesus claiming that his friend, her brother, would rise again, now. The sister, on the other hand, saying, "yes," but imagining that he would rise in the afterlife. She was sure he was gone from their presence—forever—until they met again in the afterlife.

One of the strangest relationship breakups I ever had took place in my first semester of college. I had been hanging out with a girl I was getting to know. Nothing serious yet, but it was the start of something, I thought. I liked her, but I was unsure of myself. After a few times hanging out, I felt we were moving in the right direction. Then came the fateful phone call one afternoon. After a little small talk, I said, "Hey, I was going to head over to the library and study for the next few hours. Would you want to meet me over there to hang out a bit?"

After a bit of awkward silence, she responded, "Rob, you know, I'm just thinking, I'm just not able to make any commitments right now. Is that okay?"

As I hung up the phone I was confused. Did she just break up with me? My roommate, who knew I was asking her out on this incredibly innocent "library date," saw the confused expression on my face and asked, "What happened? What did she say?"

I replied, "I think she just broke up with me."

I still remember the feelings of shock. I had asked her to join me at the library, but apparently I had pushed too hard. Maybe I had been too clingy before, this was the straw that broke the camel's back, and now she was breaking up with me. I felt incredibly rejected. Wow.

As the weeks went by, I saw that girl from time to time on campus, but I stayed away. I was hurt, and the breakup was something I wanted to put behind me. Months went by before she finally cornered me in the lobby of our dorm. "Rob, what happened? Why have you been completely avoiding me? Why won't you talk with me?"

I looked at her confused. "Because you broke up with me. I wanted to just move on."

"When did I break up with you?" She looked completely surprised.

Now I was confused. I told her about the "breakup" phone call.

"Rob, I didn't break up with you. I was only telling you I couldn't make any commitments to meet you at the library that day. You thought I broke up with you?"

Indeed I had. I had completely misinterpreted what she said. Two people, same conversation, two different understandings.

Jesus and the sister, one conversation, two people, two different understandings. Her misinterpretation of what Jesus said is plain to see. There were those who felt that Jesus' decision to not show up in time to save the man had placed a very clear limitation on him. I wonder if we don't place a similar limitation on Jesus too.

They knew Jesus could do amazing things. But their limitation on Jesus involved what we call death. They could see Jesus, and they could touch him. He looked human enough. But they had never visibly witnessed anyone reaching beyond the boundaries of our world and into another. No one would ever imagine that Jesus could reach from the here to the there. To the afterlife.

Most people of Jesus' time shared the same three "hopes" I explored earlier. They hoped that each day would unfold before them. They hoped for the future, for a life beyond this one (resurrection day, they called it). And the Jewish community in particular held out hope for "The One." They call "The One" a "messiah." To this day, active Jews still hold out hope for "The One."

But Jesus wasn't telling anyone that they would eventually see their brother or friend, Lazarus, on resurrection day.

Instead, he was going to shatter the boundaries that had been assumed about his power. He was going to blow through the walls of the people's limits. And to do that, he says something earth shattering to the mourners: "I am the resurrection (the afterlife) and the life (the here and now)" (John 11:25; parentheses are mine).

Let me rewrite this so you can see ALL three of the hopes:

Jesus then said, "I don't think you understand what I am saying. I know you believe [hold on to hope] in both the life here and the life beyond, but I need you to understand this: I AM the life here and now. I AM also the resurrection. That is, I AM the afterlife too. I AM here and I AM there. I AM in both worlds. And only 'The One' can say and do that."

It's one thing to say it. But there is only one thing he could do to prove that he could reach beyond this world to the next. And he needed his friend to be convincingly dead (four-days dead) for this to make the kind of statement he was looking for.

Jesus stepped out and told them to roll back the giant circular stone that rested in front of his friend's tomb because that's how the first part of the burial process took place in that day: in a cave with a large stone rolled in front of the opening. Those who were present balked because they knew that the smell of rotting flesh would be too much. Plus it wouldn't make any sense. This dead man had gone to the afterlife. He was out of reach. But Jesus was about to do what only "The One" could do and rock their world. Let me quote it directly from the Bible so you can see just how powerful this is:

So they took away the stone. Then Jesus looked up and said, "Father, I thank you that you have heard me. I knew that you always hear me, but I said this for the benefit of the people standing here, that they may believe that you sent me."

When he had said this, Jesus called in a loud voice, "Lazarus, come out!" The dead man came out, his hands and feet wrapped with strips of linen, and a cloth around his face.

Jesus said to them, "Take off the grave clothes and let him go."

John 11:41–44

Jesus said that he was the life "here" and the life "there." No one else can reach from the here to there without being "The One."

No one.

THE IMPOSSIBLE BECOMES POSSIBLE

This story challenges me. There are times I believe something is beyond the power of God and conclude that it's too late. Relationships have broken that I believed were beyond repair. *There is no way I could ever forgive that person,* I think.

Then I remember what Jesus did. He said he has the power beyond our power. He is "The One." That means nothing is impossible for him. Nothing.

About ten months ago a man walked up to me after a Sunday morning service in our church. He's a strong guy who works as a carpenter and contractor. He stood in front of me, staring and seemingly unable to speak. This rugged individual was fighting back tears. His voice broke. I told him it was fine and to just take a moment to collect his emotions. While he did that, my mind drifted back to months before when I first met him, on a weekend away for a group of about fifty men from our church. This guy had married a woman who already attended our church and who, after they married, wanted him to attend with her. This men's weekend, she thought, would be a great place for him to meet some guys and get plugged in to the community. As I ran through my memories of playing basketball and football with him and others that weekend, he began to speak:

"Rob, I could really use some prayer." It is normal for individuals to come up to me after church to request prayer, but I knew this wasn't easy for him to ask. I was willing to bet that it was one of the first times in his life he had ever asked for someone to pray for him. And it was hard to do. So it must've been something weighing heavily on his heart.

"What's going on?" I asked.

"Well, my wife and I are trying to have kids. We were having a difficult time so we chose to go the route of in vitro fertilization. When we met with the doctor on Friday to find out how the in-vitro process was proceeding, he told us that, upon his inspection, her ovaries looked like they were done. 'Dead,' he said. And then he told us"—at this point, my friend could no longer hold back his emotions—"that we probably would never be able to have children."

As he stood there and sobbed, I beckoned for his wife who was standing nearby to join us for this prayer. A church board member and I placed our hands on both of their shoulders and began to pray for them and this difficult situation. We prayed that Jesus, who could reach past the barriers of time and space and boundaries we had placed upon him, would reach into her ovaries and restore life to them.

I had some hope, but honestly, I was a realist. I felt like the dead man's doubtful mourners while I drove home that afternoon. I know God is powerful and that through Jesus he brought that man back from the dead, but honestly, it is harder to hope for miracles today.

Two weeks later, the man stayed after the service and talked to that same board member. No tears this time. In fact, no sadness, only excitement. He shared that the week after we prayed, they went to their follow-up visit to confirm that the in vitro did, indeed, not work. But to the doctor's shock, life had been restored in her ovaries and his wife had a very good chance of becoming pregnant. They were now very hopeful.

Four months ago the tears in their eyes were not of pain or sadness, but from joy. This six-month-pregnant-with-twins woman was really, really pregnant. I inquired a bit, and with smiles on their faces they reported that each baby was healthy and very large and things were going great.

Two weeks ago, I had the chance to see those five-pound newborns. Precious, incredible, and from the impossible to the possible. Mom and Dad, although tired, were beaming.

We have hope in our lives. We hope for the day to unfold; we have hope in the here and now. We also quietly hold on to hope for a life beyond here, a heaven that awaits us when we die. None of us have guarantees about how our day will unfold. And none of us has been to the life beyond. But "The One" has. His power extends from here to there and from there to here, and he is reaching into both worlds every single day. And that means that "The One" for me is Jesus. I do trust him. Not everything plays out the way that I want it to, and my specific dreams are not always fulfilled, but I know Jesus has the power to do whatever he wants.

All of this, of course, leads to more questions, doesn't it? As I sat by the fire pit with my friends that evening, questions about God and Jesus led to more questions. And for inquisitive people, it always works that way.

CHAPTER 7

THE IMAGE

Susan and I took our kids to Magic Kingdom at Disney World last year. As we walked through the always-busy park and took in the sights and the rides, I learned a few things. For instance, Disney employs 66,000 people, in Orlando alone, in order to keep the parks running and functioning well. Throughout the day, staff members walk through the parks recording notes about each chip of paint or loose screw or imperfect shingle and mark it down for the night crew to repair. Every single day when the gates close at night, an entire crew of cleaners and detailers flood the parks with the goal of restoring each park to its highest level. Every. Single. Day.

And that work is apparently well worth the effort because those who visit the park choose to revisit Disney several times. In fact, 72 percent of the people in the parks are repeat customers. Disney is truly a remarkable organization.

But what fascinates me even more about Disney World is that such an extensive and diverse group of people can merge together there so tightly and seamlessly. Many languages, cultures, religions, backgrounds, experiences, and races all share one relatively tight space and collectively experience the fantasy that Disney creates.

As I walked around, I watched the crowds of people interacting with and weaving amongst each other. It was incredible. And although there were obvious differences between the people, significant similarities linked us all. Probably the most obvious was the way parents cared for and tended to their children—doting, feeding, loving, smiling, and even disciplining. It is a clear cross-cultural link. Different people and cultures and religions, but caring, loving parents in each one. Somehow we're linked at Disney World, and beyond.

That's just the beginning. When you consider a similar linkage through the lens of God and his creation of humans, you have to believe that he is fully aware of our immense diversity because our creator intended us to be that way. Walking through Disney World is as close to seeing God's pronounced diversity and, for the most part, harmony, that you can ever experience anywhere.

Which leads me to a question: How does God see us in all our diversity? In other words, how does he look at us as a whole?

A previous chapter suggested your "image" is often driven by how you see yourself. Seeing yourself as Jesus sees you, as his treasure, can alter how you view yourself and how you choose to live your life. You are so valuable to him that he was willing to give up everything for you, even his life. Although Jesus and God are one, I want to separate how Jesus views us from how God views us, for what I'll be sharing here in this chapter.

How does God see you and me? He created us, yet what value are we to him? I've concluded that the answers to these questions are significant enough to shape how we live and the way we make choices in life. But it takes a little digging to figure this out, starting with the creation story that is found in the very beginning of the Bible, in a book called Genesis. It is there that we find a small verse that starts it all off:

So God created mankind in his own image, in the image of God he created them; male and female he created them.

Genesis 1:27

God made us in his image. Upon first reading this, I naturally concluded that God, then, probably looks a lot like us. Since we have arms and legs and a head, etc., then he must have those same things. "He must be something like us," was my conclusion. And that is the conclusion for most of us; we see images of God as a person on TV or in cartoons all the time. White robe, white hair, etc. Or maybe as a Hollywood actor like George Burns (*Oh, God!*) or Morgan Freeman (*Bruce Almighty*).

But I think we can all agree that there is more to God than the image of an old man in a robe leaning on a cloud with an angel fluttering over his shoulder. Deep down we believe that God has to have more depth and presence and power than the familiar pictures we've all seen. So, if the question is "How does he see us?" then maybe we have it backward; maybe he doesn't look like us at all, but rather, we look like him. But in what way? The hints are right in front of us. Like this first one.

BE CAREFUL WHAT YOU CARVE

If you grew up going to church, you are probably familiar with "The Ten Commandments." This list of "laws" is treasured by Jewish people as the final authority from God on how we are to live and interact with God and in society. For Christians, it is part of our understanding of God's expectations and standards for people everywhere. One of the particular ten that God gave to Moses is relevant to us right now, the second commandment:

> You shall not make [carve, or construct] for yourself an image in the form of anything in heaven above or on the earth beneath or in the waters below.
>
> Exodus 20:4 [added for emphasis]

This commandment can appear a bit arcane. However, when you consider that the normal practice of many cultures in the ancient world was to create, make, or carve an object to represent something to worship, it makes sense why God pushed against this. If you were to travel to the first century and the then-coastal city of Ephesus located on the north side of the Mediterranean Sea, you would discover that the city was once cosmopolitan and beautiful. You would also discover that the famous Ephesus was the city where people came to worship one of the mighty fertility gods of the Romans and Greeks. Her name was Artemis. An enormous statue was built to honor her, and it provided an idol for people to worship as they requested either bountiful families or to heal their infertility. In addition, one of the then-wonders-of-the-world, a temple, was built nearby for worshipping Artemis, and it stood close enough to the waters that ships could see the temple before anything else of the city. It was an idol to rival all idols.

This is precisely what this second commandment is telling us not to do. God is essentially saying, "I don't want you to build anything that you can worship. I don't want you directing your attention toward an inanimate object because that is not me." He's also saying, "I don't want you to try to build an image of me. I don't want you to attempt to create something that would be a likeness of me. And I don't want something put on a mantel that you consider a worship of me. Or anything placed in a public space that would drive people toward it. No, don't do it."

Why?

One could say: nothing could ever be created by human hands that could capture the beauty and massiveness of God. And if you build something to worship, you begin to worship that inanimate object instead of God, who is present everywhere. And these reasons would be true.

But I believe God told us not to create an image of him for an even more significant reason. But I can't share that without first looking at the second hint.

WHAT'S IN A NAME?

Names are powerful. When I was younger, I know I didn't appreciate the value of meaningful names. But now, having grown older and having listened to thoughtful individuals, I have gained a new respect for parents who very carefully and intentionally choose their children's names because of their meaning. For instance, Sophia means "wisdom" and Matthew means "gift of God." Names carry deeper meaning and can create value.

Names carry a weight, for good or for bad, too. The more popular or familiar a name becomes, the more that name carries with it presence, power, and the likelihood that people have opinions about it. I worked in the pro shop of a country club while in high school and college. I loved working with people and being near the golf course. Over the years, I got to know the people of the club pretty well. It was interesting to look at the schedule on any given day and see how many names I was familiar with on the tee-time schedule. But what was most interesting were the feelings I had about those names simply by looking at them. And I wasn't alone—it was a staff-wide experience. I could see that the "Johnsons" were on the list and think, "Oh, I like the Johnsons. They're always polite and thoughtful when they come into the shop. They always have smiles on their faces. Good people!"

But then I might see the "Smiths'" name and cringe. The staff cringed when we saw their name on the morning schedule because the Smiths were usually angry and bitter and always complained about something the staff did. They appeared to approach life like it was always unfair toward them. They never shared positive words of encouragement or acknowledgment. I used to think, "When people look on a sheet of paper and see my name on it, what reaction do they have? I hope it isn't like the Smiths."

Again, for good or bad, names matter. When we head back to the Bible and visit the story of a man named Moses in the book of Exodus, chapter three, we discover that some names are simply very powerful.

According to the story, Moses was chosen by God to free roughly two million enslaved Hebrews from Egypt. If you have read the account or seen some of the epic movies on this story, you know that Pharaoh ordered all the baby boys in Egypt who were born of Israelite slaves to be thrown into the Nile River in order to stem the rapid growth of the Hebrew people. In order to spare Moses' life, his mother placed him, as a three-month-old, in a basket and sent him down the river, where he was later plucked out by an Egyptian and raised within the royal household, as an Egyptian.

Years later, the Israelites were tormented by their enslavement, and Moses was aware of it. He was also aware that his true heritage was Hebrew. Upon watching an Egyptian beating up a Hebrew, Moses intervened in the situation and ended up killing the Egyptian and burying him in the sand. Word got out, and Pharaoh's men chased him. He escaped to the wilderness, where ultimately he encountered a large family of herders. He took shelter with them and eventually married one of the daughters.

More years went by. Moses found himself shepherding alone when a solitary bush ignited into flames and a voice called to him from those flames. It claimed to be the God of his Hebrew ancestors. It wanted him to go back to Egypt and free the millions of Hebrews from the grasp of Pharaoh. Moses didn't feel adequate to accomplish the task. He provided excuses for not going. When he was beginning to buckle, he challenged God with a pretty demanding request.

Susan sometimes asks me to do something, and I'll balk at first. Recently, she asked me to run to the grocery store. Neither of us find that task particularly appealing, so I balked, even though it was my day off and I wasn't doing anything. "I'm busy working on something," I yelled out to her in the other room as I watched TV.

"But, Rob, I need you to pick up these things so we can have dinner for the next few nights."

"I have to help Emma with her homework."

"It's already done."

"I'm super slow in the grocery store!" I was getting desperate.

"You can take your time," she called back.

"Well, if I go, I'm not going to be able to find everything." And when I said that, I knew I would be going. I gave my last excuse but knew I had lost this one. "Well, if I go..." was a grand signal that I was going to the grocery store. I was conceding and knew it.

Moses tried to get out of going back to Egypt. But then, as if he had nothing left to argue, he said, "Suppose I go..." (see Exodus 3:13). It was the grand signal that he'd be going. But he still threw down a desperate but valid request. "Suppose I go, who do I tell them sent me?" In other words, what is your name?

From the beginning of humankind, God had never revealed his personal name. Never said it or uttered it. He was known by more impersonal names like Elohim (generic name for God) and Adonai (a bit more personal, but still pretty generic). Moses asked for God's personal name. "If I go, I need to know your personal name. That is the only way they'll believe you sent me."

When God finally gave his name, he said it was "YHVH." A very unique and strange name. Because of its structure and the missing vowel usage of the Hebrews, this name could be described as a holy and utterly unpronounceable name. To this day, because of the oral Hebrew tradition, we have no idea how this name is truly pronounced. We use words like Jehovah or Yahweh, but we really don't know for sure.

That makes you wonder if that's not entirely unintentional by our God. Maybe it was his plan all along. Not only does he give us a name we can't actually speak, but he also told us not to construct or carve any image of him. There must be a reason. But there is one more hint we need to examine in order to know for sure.

DON'T LOOK

In yet another incident in the Bible, from the book of Exodus, we find that our main character Moses had grown closer and closer to God. He'd already led the Hebrew people out of Israel, and they were continuing their journey to a land that God promised them. On this particular exchange in chapter 33 between Moses and God, Moses requested that, since they were so close in their relationship, he be allowed to see God face-to-face. Moses, in all his exchanges with God, had yet to see him fully. Because of their journey together, Moses felt inclined to see God visibly—the next step in their relationship.

It is here that God says no. Well, not exactly, but close. Here is what he said:

> There is a place near me where you may stand on a rock. When my glory passes by, I will put you in a cleft in the rock and cover you with my hand until I have passed by. Then I will remove my hand and you will see my back; but my face must not be seen.
>
> Exodus 33:21–23

God also stated in an earlier verse that "you cannot see my face, for no one may see me and live" (Exodus 33:20).

Essentially, God is saying to Moses, "I will allow you to experience me and to know that I am there, but my actual self you are not allowed to see."

So, you can't see him, say his name, or create an image of God. Why?

THE BIGGER IMAGE

I recently finished another Dan Brown novel while on vacation (author of *The Da Vinci Code*, *Angels and Demons*, *The Lost Symbol*). Brown's foremost skill is his ability to carefully and masterfully create multiple levels of unique revelations that leave the reader wondering what all the pieces mean and how they'll all fit together in the end. He does this to create a crashing effect at the conclusion, when all of the moving parts you were holding come screaming together and one by one they all make sense. You stop and say, "Oh wow, that's why _____ happened!" He is the aces at that skill.

The three areas of the Old Testament I've just shared with you work in a very similar way. Independently, they are powerful on their own. But when you bring them together, something beautiful happens. First, we are told that we are not to create an image of God. We're not to carve one, shape one, or build one. Nor are we to find an object, make it into something, and place it on our mantels or shelves at home. It would be too limiting. But more is unfolding here than mere limitations.

Second, God gives us a name for which we have no model of pronunciation. It's a name that we no longer have in its pronounceable form, if we ever did. He's known as our father and our God, but his personal name is not in our vocabulary.

And third, when Moses asked to see God face-to-face, God told him no. However, he was able to see the presence of God as he passed by, where he had just been. We are not to see God directly.

If God doesn't want us to create an image of himself...

If God doesn't give us a name we can actually pronounce...

If God doesn't allow us to see him...

Then what is the image of God? What does it mean that

we are created "in the image of God"? What is the image of God in this world?

It's you.

You are not just made "in" the image of God, you *are* the image of God. He doesn't want us to carve an image, to fully grasp his personal name, or to try to see him directly. Rather, he's telling us that we are the living, breathing, and walking image of him. We are the presence of God in this world. We are his presence in and through all things.

You ARE the image.

When the significance of that implication begins to shake loose, it can alter how you approach your life entirely. You can choose how you will live out that image. You aren't forced. For instance, you can develop a very unhealthy and awful image that taints and misrepresents God. Or you can walk with the creator and expose the great things of God.

When I officiate at weddings, I give the couple what is called the pastoral charge. After the bride walks down the aisle with her father or someone who represents that role, and after the groom receives the bride to himself, they both turn and approach me. At that time, I give a ten-to-fifteen-minute minitalk designed for them, but the congregation is able to listen in. The passage I often choose is from Ephesians 5 of the New Testament. There the apostle Paul, when describing marriage and its incredible value, searches for something to compare it to. It's like he's saying, "Marriage is so significant, so amazing, what could I use to describe it? How about Jesus and his sacrifice for the church (the body of believers)? Yes, marriage is so amazing that it resembles when Jesus gave up his life and died for the church."

The apostle Paul actually lifts up the institution of marriage and compares it to the single most significant and profound reconciling, restorative, redeeming, and renewing event in the history of the world—the death and resurrection of Jesus for all of us. After I've described that, I look at the couple and say, "So, you two, what this means is that marriage is significant and beautiful. But it also means that when you are officially married and you walk down the aisle together, you become the walking and living and breathing picture of the greatest event that ever took place. You are the living embodiment of what Christ did on the cross for us. So how you live with each other, how you treat each other, how you talk with each other, all of it, is a testimony and an outward image of what Christ did." And then I pause just long enough to grab everyone's attention and I lightly say, "So good luck with that."

When God made us "in" his image, it wasn't that he

looked like us. Rather, it's that we are the walking and living and breathing embodiment of God. We can make it beautiful or we can present a sad image. Either way, we are his presence.

This image of God is also communal. It's not only the presentation of an individual person who is the image of God, but also the entire collected gathering of his creation. It is the picture of a region or a country. It is the image of the diversity of the world of people. A snapshot of more than seven billion people collected together shows what God really looks like. All the colors, cultures, and uniqueness are God's design of his very own image. Beautiful.

The fact that you are created as the living image of God means he values you incredibly. God is so intentional that he created you on purpose. When he did, he looked at you and said, "You, my friend, are the image of me. Go and be me."

When you embrace that, you begin to find purpose in your presence in this world and know that you matter. That is something you must embrace because it will define everything about you and your value in this world. You have enough control of your life that you can walk as God's very presence in the midst of others. That is why Jesus talked of the Kingdom of God. We can participate in it and walk in it as God's image. And when we do, we experience what Jesus means when he says, "The Kingdom of God is within you."

The creation of God's image isn't limited to an event forever ago with Adam and Eve. "Creation" is ongoing and always. The image of God is being birthed uniquely into our world all the time. It never stops. His image keeps presenting itself in the form of children and art and design and ingenuity and on and on and on.

When I look at my four children I see both the individual image and the whole image of God. When I look back at their births, although they all looked incredibly similar to each other when they were born (to each one I said, "Oh, you again," when I first held them), they stand now before me uniquely made and intentionally placed here on earth as the walking, living, breathing presence of God. Amazing.

BEING THE IMAGE

A group of six of us were at a conference in Atlanta eight years ago. After dinner one evening at a local restaurant, half of us, which included me, had to catch an evening flight. The other half were staying for an additional few days. We said our good-byes and made our way, with our luggage, out of the restaurant. Now, in the early era of cell phones, there was little very smart about them. So finding a local cab company to transport us to the airport was proving to be more difficult than I thought. I tried and tried, but from what I could deduce, this area was rarely serviced by cabs.

The only thing I could think to do was lead our little group into a nearby sporting goods store and ask if they knew any cab companies or buses or if they had a phone book. When we finally found someone to help us, she said she didn't think she'd ever seen a cab in this suburban part of the city. That wasn't good news for us. As she began to walk away to get a phone book, I heard another voice from behind me.

"Excuse me. What did you need help with?" We all turned to look toward the voice. There stood a pleasant woman whom I would guess, from the ten- and twelve year-old kids next to her, was about thirty-five or forty years old. She was smiling, not very tall, and apparently inquisitive. Her Southern accent was so sweet too. But I had been caught off guard, and I wasn't sure how to respond to her question. Our little group of three was from the northeast. In all my years there, I can't think of an instance where someone I didn't know, out of the blue, inquired about a problem I was having. This was foreign to us. So we just stared at her. (We call that Northern Charm.) I had a flash that maybe God had sent this woman to help us find a cab company. I was growing nervous and started to wonder, but then thought it would be unlikely. Silly even. She continued, "I couldn't help but overhear your conversation with the woman who worked here. Are you in need of help?"

Still shocked by her forwardness, I finally spoke up, "Well, yes . . . er . . . we're in a bit of a bind. We're looking for a cab company in the area. Do you know of any?"

"Well no, I'm sorry, I don't." She was still smiling and still looking at us.

"Okay, thanks then," I replied, already looking away for somebody else who might be able to help us.

"Where do you need a ride to?"

Why would she ask that? I thought.

Someone else in our trio responded, "The three of us were attending a conference here in town, and now we're trying, without any luck, to get to the airport."

"Follow me," she said without another question. Without knowing us at all, without thinking about who we might be, and apparently trusting us completely, she waved her arm and in a very simple but clear voice continued, "You-all will ride with my boys and me. I'll get you to the airport. No problem."

I stood there for a moment before climbing in the door to her SUV. *What just happened?* I thought to myself. After we piled into the car and were safely on our way, I began to dialogue with her. She was, indeed, a Christian and told me she listened closely to the times when God prompted her to do something. She said she suddenly felt like she should give us a ride to the airport, during rush hour, thirty to forty minutes down the highway, in the opposite direction of her home.

She didn't know us but that didn't seem to matter. She didn't care that we were from a different part of the country or that we looked different or that we might not be who we said we were. She felt God's nudging, and she wanted to be The Image. She wanted to live the way God would, for she is the living, breathing image of the creator of the universe.

This is the experience of walking in the presence of God. It is an adventure. It might be risky and it might be unknown, but when we walk as his image in this world, we get to be a part of some of the greatest things on earth.

So there I was at Disney World, looking around at all the diversity. So many cultures, religions, and nations represented. I was reminded that each person, male or female, young or old, black or white, rich or poor, and no matter where they were from, what they believed, or what they ate, were the walking, living, breathing image of God. They were intended to be here. God wanted them and you and me to be here. Imagine if we all embraced our image as God's. Imagine what would happen if we could connect ourselves with the truth that we were created that way. What are the possibilities?

And what if being the Image had more implications? What if God made us that way for a reason? And what if that reason was incredible? Let's take a look...

CHAPTER 8

NATURAL

Hello?"

"Is this Rob Strong?" the female voice asked.

"Yes, this is. Who is this?"

"This is Renee from the graduate school." She told me what department she was in, but I don't recall what it was.

I received this phone call at my off-campus apartment in the spring of my senior year of college. I was already accepted to graduate school and registered for classes the coming school year. Maybe she had questions about my schedule or, worse, payments. I wish I had asked how she had gotten my phone number. It wasn't listed in the school directory or the town phone book. I hadn't given it to the graduate school yet. To this day, I've never learned how she found me. "Okay, Renee. How can I help you?"

"I was wondering if you were going to be a preacher after you graduate?"

What? A preacher? I was now confused as I wasn't expecting that question and I wasn't sure that word defined my interest in being a pastor. I didn't see *pastor* as limited to *preacher*. I saw the pastor role more as a teacher or speaker, in addition to leading and discipling. But why quibble? I thought I knew what she meant. "Well, Renee," I replied, "I am planning to go into ministry and serve as a pastor someday."

"Great! I have a scholarship available to anyone who is going to be a preacher. If you are interested, would you come down to my office to receive the application?"

I was shocked. I felt honored but still not convinced she was contacting the right person. "Sure," I said apprehensively. "I'm busy this morning, but I can run by your office and get the application this afternoon. Is that okay?"

Later that day, as I parked my bike outside of the main graduate-school building, I didn't know what to expect. I had never received a scholarship. Some of my friends had been so effective in applying for scholarships that they had drastically shaved down the cost of their education. Maybe this was something for me to consider.

It took me a little while to find Renee's office. I had never been in this part of the building. I had not even known it existed. When I finally opened her door, her office felt almost temporary. There were few books on the shelves, and it was so straight and clean that it had the opposite of that "lived-in" feel.

"Rob? You made it! Here, have a seat," she greeted, pointing to one of the two chairs facing her nearly bare desk. She was incredibly sweet.

"Thanks," I said as I sat down. "You mentioned an application for me to pick up?"

"Oh, yes. But you know what, it's really not that long. You can just fill it out here if you want."

"Okay," I said. This didn't seem like your typical way of applying for a scholarship. I was now nervous because I wasn't ready to fill it out right now. And when I reached into my pocket for a pen, matters grew worse as I only found a worn and semidull pencil. "All I have is this pencil. Is that okay?"

"Oh, sure. No problem." She slid a yellow paper toward me. It contained the standard fill-in-the-blanks—Name, Address, City, State, etc. Beyond that, all this application contained were two simple questions:

"What are your current studies in the area of theology and ministry?"

and

"What do you plan to do with your ministry calling?"

I assumed the second was where I would emphasize my future in "preaching."

As I used my ragged pencil to fill in the blanks and answer the questions, I couldn't imagine how this all came about. An unlisted phone number, a random question about my future, a location that almost felt clandestine. Was this legitimate? Was this the strange start to my quest for more graduate-school funds? *There is no way anyone can take this five-minute application written with a pencil seriously*, I thought, sure I'd never be awarded the scholarship.

"Thanks!" she said as I slid the paper over to her. "That's it."

"Okay." I stood to leave but then, feeling a little bewildered, asked one last question. "Renee, who is providing this scholarship?"

"Oh, that's a secret. They want to remain anonymous. They've been providing this scholarship to two students each year for about ten years. That's all I can share."

"All right," I said, smiling at her. "I appreciate the opportunity. Have a good day."

"We'll be in touch!" I heard her say as I exited her office, not entirely sure I could remember how to get downstairs and out to my bike.

About three weeks went by and I had actually forgotten about the scholarship when one afternoon, the phone rang. "Hello?"

"Is this Rob Strong?" It was the familiar voice of Renee.

"Yes, this is."

"Rob, I just wanted to let you know that you were awarded the scholarship you applied for. Congratulations!"

I struggled for words because I was so surprised. "Really? Wow. Thanks."

"Okay, then. Have a good afternoon!"

I started to say a good-bye and suddenly thought to ask, "Renee?"

"Yes?"

"I was just wondering, what is this scholarship for?"

"Well, if you remember, it is a scholarship for those who are going to be preaching later in life."

"Yes, I do remember that part," I said, trying to think of another way to ask my question. Honestly, I was anticipating a few hundred dollars, which would be great for book purchases each semester. "I guess what I'm asking is what is the value of this scholarship?"

"Oh, I see. Rob, it is a scholarship that covers all of your graduate-school tuition."

I couldn't speak. My mouth hung open. Grateful she couldn't see my shock, I finally asked, "Are you serious?"

"Yes. Hadn't I told you?"

"No, I mean, I don't think so. This is for all my classes? Paid for?"

"Yes, Rob, that's what this scholarship is designed to do. Congratulations."

This event was a moment of immense clarity for me. Confirmation, actually. I felt a clearer direction pointing me toward the path I had chosen as a career and passion for my life. As a twenty-two-year-old, I didn't know much about how the world worked, but I could see the direction God was pushing me. I also had a distinct feeling that someday I would need to share and to slowly unveil things about God. That has been confirmed in many ways over and over through the years. Now, twenty years later, I am ready to share what I have discovered about God and how he works with his creation, his people.

Much of this book has already captured what I've learned over the years. But this chapter and the next are the heart of what keeps me most excited about sharing what I know about God. The experience of connecting with him and walking with him is unique for each one of us, but it requires each of us to extend ourselves to him in response. And it can change how we see God and experience life.

A friend once told me that sometimes something is revealed to you and if you don't share it, you'll feel like you'll explode. He said that is your cue to speak up. I now resonate with that more than ever. Let me explain: Over the years, I've invested countless hours working and thinking on the very things I'm sharing here in this book. What I continue to encounter outside and inside the church is that there is a fundamental understanding of our relationship with God that is missing. It really goes back to the third chapter when I asked, "If there is a God, then what does he want with us?" And I also said that if you could answer that, you will have figured out the most overlooked but most important piece of information in the entire world.

I think that missing piece has been lost in our quest to create a protected religion of "right thinking." I believe we are missing out on the beauty of what God wants for us because we've worked so hard on doing the "right things." I know that when I get a chance to speak to an audience about the things I'm writing about in this book, and especially the things I'm about to share, afterward I am often swamped with the same response: "I've never heard someone describe God and our relationship with him this way! No one has ever told this to me!" And that is usually a very specific type of audience: those already claiming to be active followers of God.

Something has been missing, and I have found it. And yes, I do now connect with my friend's words. If I don't share this, I do feel like I'll explode.

NATURAL AND UNNATURAL

What does God want from each of us? And what does God want life to be like for us and him, together? In order to begin to answer any questions like these, we need to step back in time. All the way back to the creation story found in the first book in the Bible, Genesis. It is where the stage was set for all of humankind. Whether or not you are familiar with the story of Adam and Eve, or you know it but think of it as an unreal picture of how we arrived here in this world, or you believe that God created this earth and universe in seven literal days, or you reason that the writers used the word "days" as symbolism to represent "millions of years," or you view the creation story as poetry for a much larger truth—regardless, the imagery of the creation story was intentionally used by the author of Genesis to communicate a larger truth of how we all came to exist on this earth. So consider this your very own genesis, if you will. God created man and woman in his own image. The setting was a beautiful garden, Eden.

Adam and Eve, the first two created humans, were unique in their relationship with God because of how closely they walked with God. This has significant implications for our lives today if we embrace the magnitude of that simple fact inherent in the imagery of Genesis. The idea of walking closely with God can seem like a foreign concept to us. God can feel distant from us, like the Big Guy Upstairs. It might seem that walking intimately or closely with him can appear to be only an Adam-and-Eve thing, and that it is not something available or intended for us. But maybe God does want us to have that close and intimate walk with him. If so, then what does it look like if we could see it? A great way to imagine it is to think back to the very first story available to us, to Adam and Eve and God.

Imagine what life would have been like for Adam and Eve while they lived daily in the presence of God. In order to simplify this, let's only focus on Adam, although I could focus on Eve too. Both walked with God closely. But how closely? What was life like for Adam as he lived in the Garden of Eden and interacted with God? One could say "perfect" or "boring" or "quiet" or "everything was in order and there was no disease and Adam was happy." We could suggest answers like these, but we'd be missing something. And it centers on God and Adam. Let's zoom in tighter and ask the question this way: What was an average day like for Adam and God together? Picture a day in the life of Adam and God, via hidden video camera.

What do you see? Think of it. Picture it.

Let me share first what I don't see. I don't envision a guy (Adam) who was awoken with the sound of an alarm clock because he had committed to himself that today would be different than other days. Or that he wanted to get up and set aside some time for God. I don't see a man who wanted to explore God more and be alone with him, but just doesn't have the time or the self-discipline. Neither do I see a man somewhat bored by his faith or one who lived with guilt because he knew what he was supposed to do but didn't do it or did what he shouldn't have been doing. No. This is not how Adam and God lived together.

It had to be better than that. What I see through that camera lens I think is amazing. I see someone who, upon hearing the very present voice of God, is awoken in the morning because he recognizes God's voice and responds by getting up. I would not describe that voice of God as audible. It would not need to be because Adam would respond to it naturally, mentally, spiritually, and even physically. He does so because he is so intricately, intrinsically, and intimately woven into the creator that his body, mind, and very soul respond to God's voice without it being a chore or a question. The voice of God dwelled in and through him; it was completely natural.

Adam didn't set weekly quotas for the amount of time allocated to God because it was all God's time—and his. Their relationship was all personal devotion.

Adam actually heard God's voice. Not a booming voice yelling out at him to pick up a rake or help someone in need or to be more devoted. God's voice resided in the thoughts and emotions of Adam. He knew and responded to the creator as if it were completely natural. God spoke to his creation, to Adam, through his Spirit.

Adam and God's relationship was the experience of "walking in harmony" with one another. God's designed relationship with his creation was simply natural. Walking and living with God was, indeed, completely natural. This was his intention.

A May 17, 1979, article in *People* magazine featured a number of twins who had been separated since birth without knowing it. One specific story featured a pair of twins who were born in 1940 in Ohio. These identical twins were born and immediately put up for adoption. Both couples who adopted a twin were told that the other twin died at birth. Neither twin had died, however, and as it turned out, they grew up forty miles from each other.

Ironically...

Both boys were named James.

Neither knew he was a twin.

Both were bad at spelling.

Both were great at math.

Both had childhood dogs named "Toy."

Both eventually grew up to become sheriffs.

Both bought light blue Chevys.

Both took vacations to Pass-a-Grille Beach in Florida.

Both preferred Miller Lite and Salem cigarettes.

Both suffered from migraines.

Both married a woman named Linda.

Both divorced their Linda and remarried a woman named Betty.

Both had sons whom they named James Alan.

At the age of 39, through research about their adoptions, they found each other. From the start, they described their relationship together as completely natural. Through their unique circumstances, they discovered what it means to be in harmony with someone else. The bond they felt with each other was different than any other earthly relationship they had.

Now imagine being in harmony with the creator of the universe.

Adam's entire mind, body, and spirit were one with the creator. It wasn't an effort. It wasn't a discipline. It was a "oneness" that was beautiful for both Adam and God. God was in Adam's presence, and Adam wanted the things of God. It is an extraordinary image. Again, this description could be as much about God and Eve as it is about God and Adam. The point is that there was something natural between God and his creation.

THE LINE WAS CUT

But in that same story of creation found in the book of Genesis, that image of harmony and naturalness ended. Stopped. The line was cut. The account tells us that Adam and Eve chose to step outside of that harmony and do the one thing God had told them not to do. And in their choice against God, as the story tells us, it changed their entire relationship with God. Many describe that moment as the instant that sin altered the entire picture of God with man.

Sin converted that beautiful image of harmony into twisted and distorted lives and relationships. Everything Adam and Eve had with God, in terms of the relationship I described above, was gone.

Look closely at the very first exchange between God and Adam after sin has entered the story, and you'll see something revealing:

Then the LORD God called to the man [Adam], "Where are you?"

He replied, "I heard you walking in the garden, so I hid. I was afraid because I was naked."

Genesis 3:9–10 NLT

God had called out to Adam, probably in the same way he always had, but this time it frightened Adam, and he and Eve hid. They were suddenly afraid of God. And completely aware of their nakedness. I can relate to that. When my kids unexpectedly appear when I'm not fully dressed, I dive for cover. But the reason that Adam hid when God called him was far more significant than physical nakedness. Adam's fear and decision to hide was because hearing God call him this time was a foreign experience. Before, his walk with God was natural and internal. Now he only heard God externally. Note the difference. Adam would not only realize he was naked physically, but would feel naked spiritually and emotionally. Adam would have experienced other new feelings too, like loneliness, abandonment, confusion, and disorientation. What was natural had changed immediately to unnatural.

UNNATURAL

Our separation from God is actually unnatural. We gradually grow comfortable with it, and then what is unnatural starts to feel strangely natural. Although his separation from God would at first have felt entirely unnatural and disorienting for Adam, as demonstrated when he hid from God, in due time he would adjust to that new feeling of God residing outside of him. He would grow to think it was normal and maybe even forget what it was like to walk in natural, internal harmony with God.

We are more comfortable with God at a distance. We feel it is more natural, even normal, to think of God as the Big Guy Upstairs. Upstairs, far away, hard to hear. But it's a sad picture because it's actually not natural. What was natural—to experience God internally and to walk in harmony with him—has been shifted. Life without God is viewed as natural, which makes seeking God's presence and giving God a place in our lives unnatural to the world around us. That could explain why "church" and "religion" are rejected by many in culture. The idea of walking in harmony with the creator appears ludicrous and silly.

It makes you wonder if we're not missing something.

It makes you wonder if it shouldn't be more natural or more beautiful.

When Adam chose to disobey God, the creator says that

Adam then knew both good and evil (see Genesis 3:22). In this passage "know" means Adam experiences this knowledge; he drinks it in internally—mind, body, and soul. God's treasured creation is no longer as it was intended to be. Creation's intention (man and woman living as God's image in a natural relationship with him, with one another, with oneself, and all of creation) has now become creation's distortion (sin infiltrating the fiber of all our relationships and all creation). It is a complete twisting of the original plan. Makes you wonder if the intended plan can ever be restored.

The first time I saw Susan, I was sitting in our college library reading. As I was fighting sleep, my eyes tired and drooping, I suddenly spied a group of six college women dressed in their cross-country running uniforms as they walked by. I didn't see any of their faces because of the direction they were heading, but I did notice one set of legs. My eyes followed those legs until they disappeared. I had no idea who they belonged to, but they really spoke to me. They told me I needed to meet the person they belonged to. I had no idea who that person was. I never got the chance to see her face.

A week later, I was picking up food at the campus cafeteria when I noticed three cross-country runners in their uniforms standing in line to pick up food. And there they were—those legs. I recognized them right away. I waited forever until she turned so I could know the face that came with the legs. Like an idiot, I simply stood and stared. After that, I started to notice her around campus, even when pants covered those legs. And eventually I gathered up enough courage to ask her out for a date.

What's interesting about moving forward in a dating relationship is that your confidence in the relationship is directly contingent upon what knowledge you have, or don't have, of the other person's feelings toward you. For the longest time in dating Susan, I was cautious about sharing my feelings too overtly because I feared they might not be reciprocated. That meant the relationship moved slowly until finally there were enough signals of affirmation to communicate more freely. If you don't know how the person feels or if they are intentionally cryptic with you, you will lack confidence. If they play games with you or lead you to believe they share feelings for you but then confuse you with emotional distance, you will wonder where you stand with that person or if you should continue to pursue the relationship. Uncertainty leads to a lack of confidence and growth in a relationship.

The chasm of uncertainty separating us from God makes starting a new relationship with him difficult if you don't know first how he feels about you. Everything changes and the lines of communication begin to open up when you know that he created you intentionally and that it is actually quite unnatural for you to live at a distance from him. Imagine that God had a plan all along for connecting with you. It has never been natural for you to be apart from God. Visualize how good and right it must feel to walk with God naturally. Once sin entered the creation relationship and what was natural became unnatural, God set in motion a stunning and incredible plan of restoration. He intended for his creation to be one with him again. Thousands of years, millions of people, histories of prophets, kings, nations, wars, scandals, and improbable events all led to a moment our relationship with God was reestablished.

What if we knew God's intention was to walk in harmony with creation? What if we were certain we were his treasured creation and his intentions were to be in lockstep with his people? If we were aware of his intention for us, would that change how we approach him?

Start with the knowledge that a natural relationship between God and us was his original plan. Know that he wants to restore that relationship with each of us. And then add a truly amazing ingredient—he doesn't ever force anyone to love him or walk with him. God gives us the freedom to choose or to choose not to relate to him. We can even choose to walk away from him. That's how relationships need to be. I cannot force my wife to love me. If I did, she would never be free; she would grow to resent me. She would want to leave me. I would be a horrible person. God never makes us do anything. But his arms are open wide for us to experience what is natural.

"What does God want from us?"

He wants us to walk naturally and in lockstep with him.

He wants to build a relationship with you that can alter and reshape your life. Your creator knows and understands your circumstances better than you. In your prayer and conversation with him, he leads you ever so naturally. Even, for example, in the way you look for a job or interact with your frustrating neighbor. Ultimately God wants you to walk in harmony with him, as intended in creation from the very beginning.

IS IT POSSIBLE?

How could we ever walk naturally with the God of the universe? One could argue that it seems impossible. He IS the Big Guy Upstairs. Far away and inaccessible and impersonal, right? No. As a culture, we have subtly found ways to make God seem like he's far away.

A few years ago I was having dinner with a friend. As I set the food before him, he didn't move. He stared at his dinner plate. It didn't look as if he was going to eat anything. He had lost a considerable amount of weight since the discovery of his cancer. The weight loss was not a side effect of the cancer, but resulted from his shock and sadness about having cancer. He didn't look too good. I was unsure of what to say or do in this painful silence, so I slowly picked away at my dinner.

Finally, quietly, he spoke. "What I don't understand, Rob..." He hadn't moved or looked up, and his voice was weak. "What I don't understand is 'why?'—why would God do this to me?"

It was a rhetorical question. I knew he didn't want any attempt at an answer, so I just sat and continued to nibble on my dinner.

He finally lifted his head and said, "And what I don't understand is that I thought I had a deal with God. I committed to be a good person in my work and to be good to my family, and in return he would give me a good and healthy life. But he failed on his end. I did everything right. I went to church. I gave money. I was good to my friends. I didn't break any laws. I was and am a good person. Then why the hell do I have cancer? Didn't I do enough? What more does he want from me?"

As I sat there for a moment and drank in what he was saying, it suddenly occurred to me what he was doing. It wasn't his fault. It is a common way of looking at God. He was relating to God the way one would approach a soda machine or a candy machine.

For him, the relationship between God and people was a contractual relationship.

If he put in money, he would get the treat. If he did everything he was supposed to do, in return for that sincere investment, he would receive the good life he strived to achieve. God, to him, had reneged on the deal. God had failed. He did what he was supposed to do. So where was the payback from God?

Recently, I was standing in a line at our bank. While slowly weaving through the ropes, I had a few minutes to ponder. I wondered how many people used this branch of the bank and how many branches were in this region. I don't really know anyone who works at my bank and still have to show my identification for every transaction. I realized then that the system was a contractual relationship intentionally designed for maximum efficiency in order to reach the highest number of people to receive the best possible return. It was a well-run institution that appeared to serve everyone, including me. I gave them my money, and they provided a high standard of service in return.

On my drive home it occurred to me that I experienced nearly the same system with my cell phone company. Once I signed on the dotted line, our relationship became contractual and I was placed in a system that maximized output to the maximum number of people for maximum return. I didn't know any of the people I talked to when I called to ask for help about a bill I thought I received in error a few months ago. But they were well trained to help me resolve the issue. I paid my bills, and they provided the service.

As I pulled into my driveway, I sat there for a moment because it struck me that I have that same relationship with my electric company, my cable company, and my natural gas company. My mind stretched a little further, and I realized that my doctor's office, my satellite radio company, our local department of motor vehicles, and the local Sears all functioned on the same contractual premise. It is how our culture functions. Even my experience with the schools my children attend is that they also function on the model of high efficiency for high return.

This contractual system shapes our culture. Without even realizing it, I choose to "invest" in my family with the same construct. I look for opportunities to have quality time with each child in the family for the greatest return on investment, meaning that they will grow up healthy, respectful, and have large dreams. I assume that they will be stronger, smarter, and better because of my investment. That's the logic that seeps into my thinking.

Does this strategic and contractual thinking influence the way I see and interact with God? Yes. My solution-oriented and greater-returns culture shapes the lens through which I perceive and relate to my God. Therein lies a problem. God, who wants to be in a natural relationship with me, to walk in harmony with me, has quietly morphed into a distant CEO who works in another city far away, seventeen stories up in an office building. He doesn't feel close to me; rather, to me he feels far away and inaccessible. I struggle to believe it is possible to walk with him naturally, in harmony. That perception then shifts: if I need anything of God, I can go to the local branch (church) and talk with a teller there (pastor or priest). If I'm not careful to be conscious of the cultural shaping in my mind, God can become so distant that my interaction with him will be almost entirely contractual and results based, like approaching a candy machine and expecting a return on my deposit.

We often expect the same thing regarding the Bible. We look at the size of it and pause, for it's big and has many, many pages; little of it reads like a riveting paperback novel. Although it does contain interesting stories, history, and teachings, it's still an enormous amount of information and can't be devoured in just a few sittings. So we look at it and ask, "Could someone break it down for me into a simpler form and then let me know what I need to know and what I need to do so that I can get the maximum amount of information from the minimum amount of input and still be in good standing with God? Could someone reduce it to the important parts for me?" In my years serving in ministry, I have regularly encountered the concept of reducing the Bible to the "main points." It is a very common approach to God. We want faith simplified so we can do what needs to be done, put it behind us, and move on to the next thing. And if we do that, it functions as a contractual relationship more than a true and healthy relationship between us and God.

"What does it take to be in good standing with God?" is a question asked when we believe God is distant and detached, but ever watchful and vindictive.

FINDING THE NATURAL

It has been my experience that when God offers a truly natural, intimate, close, personal relationship to his creation (us), the tendency is not to trust him, but instead to trust our contractual candy machine and systematized God. We don't really want the systematized God. And we don't believe it is a flattering view of him. But it is the default setting for many of us in our relationship with him.

A distant, candy-machine God.

Is God really like that? Did he create that image of himself, or is that an image we created of him? Is that image of him more unnatural than natural?

Letting God speak for himself via the Bible, this is an image he wants us to have of him:

> For I am the LORD your God who takes hold of your right
> hand and says to you, Do not fear; I will help you.
>
> Isaiah 41:13

No, God does not need to be relegated to the outer edges of our lives, like a peach tree hidden in the distant weeds. He wants to walk, hand in hand, in harmony with you. Now. He's not asking for you to perform certain feats or behave a certain way. He wants you to know him for who he is. He's not in a high-rise office running things from afar. No, he wants to be in your life.

There are incredible hints of this found in the Bible. One particular individual, Paul, made a point to tell of this kind of God to people who had no Jewish background. In fact on one occasion, Paul traveled to the Roman city of Athens. Here Paul spoke to an educated, philosophical, and spiritual group of people who had no idea or frame of reference as to who Jesus was. This audience was raised on the words of Aristotle and Plato. They were sharp, pragmatic, and critical—much like people in our culture today. To help them better understand the bigger picture of the universe and how God intended things to be, Paul spoke to the crowd with these revealing words:

> God did this [sent Jesus] so that men would seek him and
> perhaps reach out for him and find him, though he is not

far from any one of us. "For in him we live and move and have our being." As some of your own poets have said, "We are his offspring."

Acts 17:27–28

By looking at the first sentence, we know Paul understands that in the Roman and Greek culture, they believed that many gods exist in the celestials (up above). The entrance of the gods in their world was often marked by great conflict and war. So when Paul described a "god" (our God) who is "not far from any one of us," he redefined the familiar image of a distant, unsympathetic, and demanding god. He introduced, instead, the revolutionary concept of a God who loves each person and is actually very, very near to each one of us.

To really drive home his point, he also quoted a familiar poet's writing to describe God: "We are his offspring." What a picture. A father who loves his children. Paul says, "For in him we live and move and have our being." This is walking naturally with our God. We live and breathe and move and think and share and love with God present.

"What does God want?" He wants us to reach out our hand and heart and tell him that we want him in our lives. No matter how rough or tough or battered we might be, he wants to relate to each of us. It feels like he might be far away, but as Paul said, "He is not far from any one of us."

Instead of running religion from a faraway tower, he explodes through our mental construct, straight into hands held out for him.

Our culture has experienced God like he is a distant candy machine. So embracing God as a part of yourself is an incredibly difficult image to accept. And walking with God naturally means you place control of your life in the hands of another—God. Countless people I've met over the years have fought this surrender. It can be scary. But it is possible.

Let me show you what it looks like in the next chapter.

CHAPTER 9

SO HE DID

Two months into my first year of college I had an opportunity to go home for a weekend to visit my mom and dad (this "dad" here is my stepfather whom I referenced earlier. I will tell this story with the same name I called him then and now, "Dad."). Since I attended school in another state, I knew this visit was one of only a few I'd get that year. I remember the feelings I had about seeing my old friends from high school and telling them my stories and what I was up to.

I remember my mom gave me a big hug when I arrived home. She was so excited. But I didn't have time to waste; I had friends to see, and I told my parents I was going out shortly, right after dinner.

"So, you are staying for dinner?" my mom inquired.

"Yeah, but it's gotta be fast. A bunch of us are going out." I was looking forward to seeing my friends.

That's how the whole weekend went. Me running to and from activities and events. And my parents looking for stories and information on my first months of college that I could not share for lack of time.

About a week after I returned to school and was back into my routine, I received a letter. As I pulled it from my mailbox, I quickly recognized the blocky handwriting. It was from my dad. *That's odd*, I thought. *Usually Mom writes me letters.*

I held it for a moment and looked at it. For him to write me meant something was wrong. I quickly headed outside to find a private place to read it. I found an empty bench, away from crowds of students, sat down, and opened it.

Dear Rob,

I'm sitting on a park bench outside of town. I have been praying about writing this letter for days. It is the hardest thing I've ever had to write. But God is nudging me to share these thoughts, and I want to be obedient to him.

Rob, your visit last weekend was not good. I watched as your mother was hurt and devastated over and over all three days. She planned for weeks for your trip here. She made all your favorite meals, moved events to be available, and wanted to spend time with you. But you never noticed or even found the time to connect. She was very, very hurt.

Son, this is hard to write. What I'm saying is that your mom doesn't want you to come home because she doesn't want to be hurt like that again. And I want to protect her from that pain.

So I will leave it to you to consider your future visits home, and I want you to consider hers and my feelings. We love you and always will, but we don't want to be treated like that again.

Love, Dad

I stared at the letter in my hand. I felt like I had been punched in the stomach, and I thought I was going to be sick. How could I have been so thoughtless? How could I have hurt my mom like that? Wanting to fix the situation, I ran back to my dorm room, sat down at my desk, and began to write her. I apologized and confessed my insensitivity and said I now knew that I had hurt her and would never want to do that again. I mailed it that same day to make sure she received it quickly. Then I decided I couldn't wait two or three days for the letter to arrive, so I picked up the phone and called. When she answered, I shared all my thoughts from my letter and even more. I was practically crying as I told her how sad I was for hurting her in such an insensitive and selfish way.

Of course she accepted my apology and gracefully forgave me. But in my years of returning home from college, graduate school, and after I moved out East to work, I never forgot the message my dad sent me. It was a game changer for me. It had revealed to me a side of myself I wasn't happy to discover. It changed how I relate to people, to this day.

Over the years, I wrestled with something else my dad wrote in his letter. It was subtle, but it amounted to much of who he is as a person. He said, "God is nudging me to share these thoughts, and I want to be obedient to him." God was nudging him? In other words, he felt he needed to write me because he felt that God was encouraging him to do so.

The more I thought about those words, the more my memories flew back to countless times in my life Dad had said those exact words. They even took me back to a specific day in my teenage years when I had suddenly awakened at 4:15 in the morning. As I struggled to go back to sleep, I saw a faint light coming from around the corner. I decided to investigate, and as I made my way down the hall, I noticed the light was coming from our family room. A bit nervous, I cautiously walked to the kitchen so I could get a better look. I discovered something profound—there was my dad, on his knees, leaning into the big chair, praying. I stood there for a second, and the mental snapshot was stored in my brain. My mom had told me that he got up every morning for a time with God, but I didn't know it was in the family room and so early in the morning. Every single day.

With that picture of my dad praying serving as a backdrop, I recalled the many times he told me he had responded to God's nudging. He would say it when he contemplated purchasing or not purchasing things. He would say something like it when I asked for permission to go to a party the coming weekend or out with friends. "I'll pray about it and get back to you, Rob." Then his answer might look like this, "Well, God is nudging me to say no about that, Rob. I hope you understand." And because of the backdrop, I knew he didn't just say it—he had prayed about it, for real. After receiving that difficult letter from my dad, I never questioned what he wrote because I knew he was nudged by God. And that's because I know what went into those words. His life, to this day, models his obedience to that nudging.

JUST HIM?

The question I had, however, was could I ever experience that communication with God in my own life? Is that something that we all can experience? I've learned that we certainly can, in many forms. A number of years ago I was at an event that featured author and speaker Eric Metaxas. He told his personal story of how he discovered God as a young man through his years of fishing and then one night encountering a unique dream that included fish and God. Yes, God spoke to him that way. He then shared that God reveals himself to each person in a language or way that each person understands. That resonated with me because I realize how God nudges my dad or whispers or speaks in dreams to someone else in a way that makes sense to the recipient. It is really the recipient who needs to be listening for that voice or whisper or nudge.

What is it like to hear God? In my dad's case with me, it was a deep conviction that he felt. He was unsettled about my visit, and so he prayed about it. Or, in my simple terms, he talked about it with God. In that dialogue, as he told God about his unsettled feelings, he would think about how to resolve the situation. That time alone with God made space to hear God and get clarity on the situation. He then knew he had to write to me. Although it would be very hard to do, he felt a unique confirmation or peace from God that to write to me was the right course of action.

In addition, when God "nudges" or affirms or directs, the results are never, ever singular. They actually have a lasting and wide-reaching effect that makes them different from the results of decisions made instinctively. My dad's letter altered the way I see my mom and visit home, even to this day. It also altered how I come home each evening to my family. I genuinely hear their stories of what they've done that day. My wife might want my attention, and although my instinct is often to seek my own satisfaction, I fight that urge because I've learned it will negatively affect my relationship with her.

Experiencing God and walking in harmony with him can be as natural as breathing. Those "nudges" can become less unique and more natural as you begin to "hear" God in more natural ways. It needn't be something that makes others cringe when they hear about it because it's so sensational they don't know what to do with it. No. And it needn't be so profound that we call it something like "Signs and Wonders." It is as natural as breathing. As beautiful as breathing.

How is that possible?

THE PLAN ALL ALONG

In the previous chapter we talked about the presence of God in Adam's and Eve's lives. Their ability to walk in harmony with God in a way that was natural. Was Adam walking directly with an old man, or was it something else that connected them in their relationship? Indeed there was. God communicated with Adam through his spirit, known as the Spirit of God. This presence was in and through Adam. So when I say that God was present in and through Adam, I am not proposing that the creator of the universe is so tiny that he fits inside of Adam. (As I'm typing this, my mind jumped to science-fiction movies of tiny people who are inside larger people, controlling them from the inside. That is NOT the image of God I want to portray here.) No. Rather, it is the presence of God through his own ever-present Spirit. In the Christian faith we talk of the Father, Son, and Holy Spirit, which make up what we call the Trinity. It is that very same Spirit that connected God to Adam so directly. It is through God's Spirit that his presence dwelled in and through Adam.

I share this because when sin distorted the world, the indwelling of God in Adam—the Spirit—was removed and with it, natural communication with God. The relationship no longer was the same, as I noted in the previous chapter.

What is so fascinating is that no one in the Old Testament interacts in the same, unique and natural way that Adam did with God, through his Spirit. Those days were gone.

So essentially, what was lost in the choices made by Adam and Eve during the creation event was harmony and naturalness with God. It was a friendship. It was family. It was God and his creation. His Spirit was removed, no longer dwelling in his people, so there was no harmony and naturalness with God.

Directly after that loss, God set in motion the greatest story of restoration, reconciliation, renewal, and redemption in the history of the world, a story that expands over thousands of years. In the Old Testament, the Spirit didn't dwell within people like it did with Adam, but it didn't disappear entirely either. There are a couple of incredible instances that ultimately reveal significant foreshadowing for you and me.

MEMORABLE MOMENTS

For instance, there is a person featured in the Old Testament of the Bible named Samuel. He served the roles of prophet and judge on behalf of God for the Israelites. They didn't have a king to lead them at that time. Instead, they used men like Samuel. But the people grew weary of being led by a prophet and judge, for they noticed that other nations around them had fearsome kings. So the people petitioned Samuel and God for a king. God allowed this, and Saul was chosen to become the very first king of Israel. Samuel was commissioned to anoint Saul as king on behalf of God (picture Chief Justice Roberts of the United States Supreme Court swearing in Barack Obama as president on Inauguration Day). During Samuel's "swearing in" ceremony of commissioning, Samuel told Saul something incredible:

> The Spirit of the LORD will come powerfully upon you . . . and you will be changed into a different person.
>
> 1 Samuel 10:6

You and I know this change that Samuel refers to is not a literal and physical change. Instead, it is a spiritual and emotional and empowered leadership transformation. This verse, therefore, hints at how powerful the Spirit of God is. It can transform the very core of a person, should they allow the Spirit of God in their lives. However, this verse also reveals that this kind of personal experience with the Spirit of God is limited to only a few human beings throughout the entire Old Testament years. This gives rise to the question: will that ever change?

In another Old Testament event, Moses was instructed by God to bring seventy of his leaders together in one location so that God could bring his Spirit upon them. I'm not sure what that looked like, but what we do know is that when it was time for the Spirit to come upon the group, sixty-eight men were there at the location ready to go. But two were missing. They didn't get the memo or information about said meeting. That didn't stop God, and the Spirit of God came upon those sixty-eight men and... amazing things happened. They were, again in reference to Samuel, changed temporarily into different people.

And, interestingly, those two who didn't make it to the leadership gathering—the Spirit of God still dropped upon them too, right where they were in the middle of six hundred thousand unaware soldiers. That freaked the soldiers out, and they sent a guy running to Moses with the report that these two men were being disruptive and that he needed to stop them. Moses didn't nod his head and acknowledge the problem, nor did he remove the two men. He looked at them and shared these incredible words:

> But Moses replied, "...I wish that all the Lord's people were prophets and that the Lord would put his Spirit on them!"
>
> Numbers 11:29

In essence, Moses said, "I wish EVERYONE could experience the presence of the Spirit of God being put upon them, but they can't."

Note the two very significant realities in these stories: First, the Spirit of God has enormous impact in the lives of people in the Old Testament. But at the same time, that impact is limited to only a few people. Only a very few people ever witnessed or experienced it.

The Old Testament shift from the Adam-and-God relationship to the stories of Moses and Samuel and Saul is significant. No longer do people walk naturally with their God. No longer is it as harmonious and beautiful as breathing. No, it is a limited blip on the screen of humanity that only a few were privy to see and experience. And Moses' words summed it all up perfectly. "I wish EVERYONE could experience the presence of the Spirit of God."

A FUNNY THING HAPPENED ON THE WAY TO RESTORATION

And then Jesus entered the scene.

From his birth through his childhood and into his adult years, there was something special about him. We are privileged to peer into one particularly significant event—his baptism.

The Spirit of God, referred to as the Holy Spirit in the New Testament, publicly came to rest upon Jesus on the day he was baptized. And that action initiated his three-year ministry. The things that Jesus did during those years would have made the writers of that day wish they had video cameras to capture it all. He healed hundreds of ailing and sick people. He restored sight to the blind and hearing to the deaf. His presence triggered thousands to follow him, just to witness some of these miracles. And as I reflect on this unique power that shook a region, I can almost hear the very same words of Samuel as he anointed Saul to become King of Israel: "When the Spirit comes upon you, you will be changed into an entirely different person."

As Jesus began to draw crowds by the thousands, because they wanted to witness what had never, ever been seen before, these gatherings paved the way for Jesus to teach how religion fell short of God's intention of a natural and beautiful relationship with us. Following the rules and the laws and the processes generated a complex system that, in the end, missed the whole point of what God wanted with us. One can only imagine how much this kind of teaching upset the apple cart of religious leaders that day, for their culture was one that was dictated and led by religious leaders. So it was through this kind of provocative teaching about what religion is not supposed to be, and through many stories and parables, that Jesus began to shake the entire cultural and religious system. What he was promoting was an end to the way of life that people knew and understood. Their theocratic society need not continue.

And I wonder: in what ways have we fallen back into religious trappings? If Jesus were to appear here today and walk through our churches and see our prolific systems, what would he say? How would he assess our . . . progress?

But take note here. When Jesus received the Spirit of God, at this point it had been given to him only. The Spirit of God was no more present in the lives of the people of that day than in Old Testament days. Only Jesus walked in the natural and harmonious presence of God. That is what made him so unique and why so many were drawn to him. He was unlike any other living person. And you can now hear those foreshadowing words of Moses some 1400 years earlier: "I wish EVERYONE could experience the presence of the Spirit of God." Is the presence of Jesus and the Spirit that lived within him a picture of things to come for all of us? Is this the picture of what the restoration of our relationship with God looks like? Maybe this is why Jesus came. Maybe he came to restore all people to God by means of the Spirit of God.

After three years, the tension between the regionally controlling religious leaders and Jesus reached a boiling point. He was undermining their power, and for them, it had to stop. At the opportune time, they rallied people against him, arrested him, and scheduled him to be put to death. Jesus knew it would happen and told his disciples at a dinner just a night or two earlier that he would be killed. Although he revealed this to them, and although the Old Testament predicted the one who came as the "Messiah"

would be put to death, it still came as a shockingly cata-
clysmic event to all who were associated with Jesus. Then
Jesus rose from the dead and walked among his disciples
and others for a few weeks. As an old African-American
preacher beautifully said, "Death couldn't hold him!" It's
the reason we celebrate Easter. In Christian history, Jesus'
death and resurrection mark the point when the shift of all
things took place. But was it? Were things complete at that
time?

I would propose here that there was still something missing. The story wasn't complete. The full restoration of us
to God was not yet complete.

I started to notice it when I read the New Testament
gospels—Matthew, Mark, Luke, and John. I noticed that,
as Jesus taught and communicated, he unnerved many,
many people, including, of all people, his disciples. As a
Jew, he challenged people to love their enemies, care for
those who weren't Jewish, and care for the poor. He lived
and dined with the outcasts of their society and cared for
those whom the religious leaders saw as the problem. In
the midst of all this upheaval, one would think that Jesus'
disciples would be the first to understand him. They traveled with him, lodged with him, and spent countless hours
with him. And yet, when you read the whole record, they
really didn't have a clue about the bigger picture Jesus was
proposing. They were just as taken aback as everyone else

by what he was saying. Confused, they would ask for extra clarification when they were alone with Jesus because they simply couldn't fully comprehend what he was saying.

I sometimes ask Christians what they believe is the moment when we were able to reconnect with God. "When Jesus died and rose again," is often the answer. I agree that that is part of the story. However, if you look closer, you will discover something quite interesting.

THE MISSING PIECE

After Jesus had risen from the dead (Christians celebrate this as resurrection) and was spending some time with his disciples, they naturally asked many questions. Wouldn't you? Of course they would, for there is always something to learn from a guy who died and rose from the dead. There would clearly be a consensus that Jesus was most definitely from God. But when you move past the stories of the resurrection and look at the Bible book of Acts, when the writer provides a glimpse into Jesus' final moments with his disciples before he left them permanently, you find something that illuminates so much of what I'm proposing here. In the book of Acts, chapter one, the writer reveals that nothing has really changed for the disciples—yet. Jesus was resurrected, yes, and they were happy and thrilled. The resurrection confirmed who Jesus said he was. But were the disciples themselves changed? No. In fact, nothing had changed in the lives of anyone— yet. And then came an incredibly simple question from his disciples—his closest followers—that reveals everything:

Lord, are you at this time going to restore the kingdom to Israel?

Acts 1:6

Having lived with the Messiah for three years and having watched him heal dozens, hundreds, maybe even thousands, and having heard him teach for hours and hours, specifically about the Kingdom of God as something intangible, unlike a building or a monarchy, the disciples still didn't get it.

"Are you now, finally, going to take back the kingdom from the mighty Romans and restore it for Israel?" What the disciples are really asking is, "So, are you going to set up your kingdom now? You've proven through your death and resurrection that you are the Messiah and so you not only have the power to establish yourself as the king of our people, but you could even establish yourself as the king over the whole Roman Empire. You're going to do that, right?"

They didn't understand. And to add emphasis, I would

propose that they didn't understand Jesus, what he was there for, just what he was doing, and the implications of his death and resurrection. They didn't understand him at all. And I would also propose that the reason they couldn't understand all these things was because...

...they weren't able to.

Because this point is so vital to the whole story, let me stress that again: The disciples who followed Jesus were not able to comprehend the reason that he had come and then died and rose from the dead. And I would propose that they couldn't understand because they had nothing to help them understand that he had come to restore things to their natural order. They couldn't understand the full implications of Jesus dying and rising from the grave. And they couldn't understand that he had done this so that all of humankind could step away from an unnatural relationship with God (that is, understanding God as just the Big Guy Upstairs...distant, irrelevant) and into the natural, walking, living, breathing, Adam-and-Eve-like relationship with God. They were closer to Jesus than anyone on the face of the earth, and they still couldn't understand his purpose for being there. And if things stayed like that, then how would anyone else be able to understand all of this? Soon, however, Jesus' disciples would understand. The key is found in Jesus' words here:

Do not leave Jerusalem, but wait for the gift my Father promised.

Acts 1:4

The gift is none other than the Spirit of God, the Holy Spirit.

I can almost hear the words of Samuel echoing from centuries before, "You will change into a different person when the Spirit of God comes upon you..."

And I can hear the ancient words of Moses too: "I wish everyone could experience the presence of God's Spirit."

Samuel and Moses knew that the presence of the Spirit of God was a rare and treasured event. For every person who came after Adam and Eve, that kind of communication and communion with God was only available in limited and special moments. That would be how the disciples would understand the Spirit of God too. They couldn't piece together that the reason for Jesus' presence on earth was to change the topography of spirituality. They couldn't understand that Jesus' death and resurrection paved the way for the coming Spirit of God. As far as they were concerned, Jesus was here to set up a monarchy for the Jews. And so, I am proposing that the disciples did not comprehend Jesus' words because they couldn't. No one, in fact, could.

But about a week later, they did.

Everything that was lost when Adam and Eve sinned was restored.

Immediately.

The book of Acts, in chapter two, captures the details of the Spirit of God arriving to the waiting disciples. They didn't know what to expect. They were simply waiting because Jesus told them to wait in Jerusalem. How could they know? But then, the disciples received the presence of the Spirit of God, just like Jesus had, just like Samuel said Saul would, just like Moses said he wished everyone could. The writer of the book of Acts describes the event as one in which the sound of something like thunder caused an enormous stir for many people in the city. The event was so monumental, thousands of people in the city came running to where the disciples were staying. They stood outside to find out what the commotion was. Remember, unlike our cities today in which cars, trucks, cranes, horns, and many other noisemakers drown out most distinct sounds, a city like Jerusalem would be relatively quiet. So, as human nature continues to prove, if there is a significant commotion, people will come running. And they did in Jerusalem.

Eventually the disciples exited their abode while people stood and watched them. Waiting. And then one of the disciples known as Peter stood up and boldly began to speak, as did the other disciples. It is significant that Peter spoke because Jesus always seemed to position Peter as a leader in the group. But during Jesus' trial and eventual death, Peter was a coward and pretended not to know Jesus. Now this coward had turned into the leader he was called to be, and he spoke first and powerfully to the many, many people who were watching and wondering. Some of the other disciples actually spoke in different languages for the visitors in the city. Others spoke the native language. But Peter stood out as the leader and began to tell the story of Jesus and the restoration of the relationship between us and God that had been lost. He was explaining the very things that did not make sense before this moment. But now he understood fully. Now it was clear. It was all clear. Peter could now SEE. His first words to the thousands of people gathered outside were a quote from a familiar Old Testament writer. They bring us full circle back to Adam and God:

> In the last days, God says, I will pour out my Spirit on all people.
>
> Acts 2:17

This transformation had a powerful effect on the people who were there. And beyond. Something fundamental had changed. Simply put, that which was lost was now made available. As Peter told us, God wants to pour out his Spirit (the Spirit of God) upon his people. And it was no longer available to only a few; instead, it was available to everyone there. So, within days, thousands upon thousands of people in Jerusalem came to embrace the story and message of Jesus and the restoration and renewal of what was lost—the natural-as-breathing walk with the creator of the universe, God. What was lost has been restored. What was destroyed has been renewed. A day the world had waited centuries for has finally dawned. Let the renewal begin!

SO HE DID

The presence of the Spirit of God (or Holy Spirit) caused a significant change in the history of the world. Now, instead of humankind living unnaturally apart from God and there being occasional stories of the Spirit of God dropping into the landscape here and there (like Samuel, Saul, and Moses from the Old Testament), the new natural was now immediately available to the disciples, the crowds in Jerusalem, and beyond. For instance, the writer of Acts recorded the travels of one of the first Christians, Philip, in the eighth chapter. This story captures a glimpse into the little-known world of one individual who was now a different person because of the natural walk he had with God. He had transformed because of the presence of the Spirit of God in his life. And he now shared that message of Jesus to others, explaining to anyone who would listen that Jesus brought restoration and renewal through the Spirit of God. After several interactions with locals in Samaria (a region and a people group normally despised by the Jews in that day), he is "called" by God to go south.

The story of Philip listening to God's "nudge" is one of the first instances where we witness someone walking in harmony with God again. No instruction manual or GPS tells him where to go. A man named Philip wants to follow God. He wants to walk naturally with him so badly that he was willing to go wherever that "voice" or "calling" or "nudge" would take him. This voice wasn't telling Philip to "go south" to do business there or meet with someone. God told Philip to go south, down a certain road, and that's it. Nothing more.

Countless times in my ministry I have encountered people who feel they are called to go somewhere beyond where they were. A "nudging from God," they would say. Then fearful and doubtful thoughts crept in, usually related to money. Many use money as the confirmation to act or not act. "If the money is there, that is our word from God to go." I recently talked with a man and his wife whose lives are committed to teaching leadership to Christians all over the world. He is currently a professor at a graduate school, but he told me that when the call to "go" arises, more than ninety percent of the time, he has agreed to go knowing that the funds weren't yet in place. In every single trip, ninety-six in total, the money miraculously arrived.

We struggle between going and doing what God wants us to do and what we think is safe and responsible. God is not irresponsible. He wants us to trust him. He knows more than we do.

So there was Philip. God tells him to go south. As we read this, imagine you're seeing this in movie form. What will he do? He has a really good thing going in Samaria. People are hearing the good news he's sharing, and he's having a significant impact in that region. Then God tells him to go south. It would make sense for Philip to say, "Not now. Things are just beginning to work here. I don't think it would be smart for me to change gears after all this time. No, I will stay here." But instead, here is what he does:

> Now an angel of the Lord said to Philip, "Go south to the road—the desert road—that goes down from Jerusalem to Gaza." So he started out...
>
> Acts 8:26–27

In the earlier version of the New Living Translation, it simply said that Philip's response was this: "So he did." I love that directness. I love the simplicity of it.

No questions. No complaining. This brief exchange lets us see the new world order. The new way of doing things with God. But it's not really new, is it? Rather, the old, old, old way is back. And it's for everyone.

Philip made his way south down the road and honestly had no idea why. Is that an adventure or what? As he was walking, he encountered a man riding in the back of his chariot, reading. God told him to go over and talk with the man. Philip didn't have a clue why, but he did it. Or should I say, "So he did."

As the story concludes, the man was so moved by the story of Jesus and the Spirit of God that he asked if he could be baptized in a small pool of water along the road. He wanted to be baptized right then.

Philip didn't know why he was called. He was walking in the living and breathing beauty of God's Spirit again. The natural way of doing things is back, and it is for all of us. The ability to walk in harmony has been restored. The "voice" or the "nudge" can be as overt as shifting one's family from one coast to the other, or even to another country. It can be as outlandish as surprising someone with an unexpected financial gift. It can be as crazy as leaving one job to go to another one. As simple as turning your car around to go home and apologize to your spouse. As life changing as a father feeling nudged to send a letter to his son who needs to be reminded to respect his mother.

The nudges are not calls to destroy families or hurt others. Never. They are calls to share, give, encourage, challenge, and even help reveal something to someone who forgot.

Is it possible for all of us? Yes. We all sit on the edge of a "so he did" moment at any time. You probably can think of times in your life that you felt the nudge to go for something that was out of the ordinary or outside of your current plans. You wanted to leap, but fear gripped you. If you think about it right now, you know what I'm talking about. More than likely, that was a "so he did" opportunity or calling or nudging staring you right in the face.

DON'T GO SOUTH, GO NORTH

A number of years ago I spent some time with a hero of mine, an author I greatly respected and had invited to speak at a conference we were hosting. In our private dialogue I had many questions, as would be expected in a conversation with someone you really respect. By the end of our time together, he invited me to join him and a few others that coming spring for a small retreat down the Atlantic coast in Maryland. I was humbled and incredibly excited. I couldn't imagine what three days with him and these other men and women would be like. I couldn't wait.

Five months later I was packing my bag for the next

morning's drive south to the retreat. Susan, simultaneously, was packing for her trip up north to stay with her parents while I was gone. She was also towing along our then three small children, ages six, three, and one. She smiled at me as she caught me staring at her. If there is one thing, among many, that I appreciate about Susan, it is her support. She knew this was a rare opportunity, and she wanted to help make it possible for me to go.

That night I set our alarm to wake me at five the next morning. The plan was that I would rise, shower, finish packing, and then wake her thirty minutes later at five-thirty. Then we would each pack our separate cars and pull out at six—she would go north, I would go south.

When the alarm went off, our room was already filled with early morning sunlight. I lay there for a few moments, contemplating the day ahead. Suddenly the oddest thought formed in my mind: "Rob, don't go south, go north with Susan."

I shook my head because the thought was so random and off my current train of thought that I wasn't sure what had just happened. It was as if someone had inserted a file in my mind with "Rob, don't go south, go north" and hit "play." I lay there thinking it was a passing thought. Just when I was about to sit up, the idea came back even more pronounced. "Rob, don't go south, go north with Susan."

I knew this voice. It was the sound of my voice in my

mind. It wasn't an audible noise in the room around me, but it was just unique enough to remind me of the scene from *Field of Dreams* when Kevin Costner heard, "If you build it, they will come." It was a distinct and unique-enough moment that it caused me to pause. This thought was natural enough that it didn't scare me. It felt familiar. It felt spiritual. So I actually responded to the thought and asked, "What?"

"Rob, don't go south to the retreat, go north with Susan."

Then I began to panic a bit. I had really planned this trip and already paid the fees. I was not happy. So I formed another question in my head: "Why? Why should I go north instead of to this incredible opportunity that is south? Why?"

The response was quick and clear as a bell, "Because Susan is tethered to you, but not nearly as closely as you think." I knew exactly what those words meant the second I heard them. Susan had been supportive of things happening in my life with work and travels, but I had been wondering if it was taking a toll on her. I had a feeling that she may be putting up a good front to be the support I needed, but was privately growing weary. "Not as closely as you think." It only confirmed my suspicions.

Then I knew this was not just in my head. From deep down in my heart, I knew this voice was true and right and from God. I knew it, but hadn't wanted to face the reality. My life in the previous few years had picked up a lot of steam with career opportunities. All the while, we were having babies. Susan never, ever stopped me. She encouraged me, prayed for me, and helped me. I had traveled internationally several times, teaching and speaking. I had accepted invitations at camps, conferences, and churches, and each required me to travel alone or arrange for my family, which included three very small children, to travel with me. It was always difficult and stressful, even when we tried to mix in a stop at Disney or the beach. When I'm completely honest with myself, I know I was pursuing what I wanted for me. I know I didn't have the right motives when I accepted those invitations. I wanted to make a name for myself. That is not the motivation I ultimately want to drive me. The more selfish the pursuit, the more damage I leave in my wake. That has always proven true.

I received an invitation to travel with a group to Rwanda for two weeks of meeting with individuals, organizations, and churches after genocide had ravaged the nation some nine years prior. I had never been to Africa, and this was an opportunity I didn't want to miss. I had kissed Susan good-bye and hopped in the car headed to the airport. As I looked back over my shoulder, I could see her waving with her left arm because she was holding an infant in her right. I rationalized. She would be fine. Besides, this opportunity only comes once in a lifetime.

Nine months prior to that trip I had been invited to India for several weeks. The trade-off for that powerful experience was I had to kiss my then-pregnant wife and two small children good-bye. It was a once-in-a-lifetime opportunity, I had told myself. They'll be fine, I rationalized.

"Because Susan is tethered to you, but not nearly as closely as you think." I lay there contemplating those words. Ten minutes had gone by. I still had twenty minutes, enough time to win the argument in my head, take a quick shower, get the final parts of my bag together, and then get Susan up. I could still make this plan come together. *This is crazy*, I thought. *Why shouldn't I go? It's a once-in-a-lifetime opportunity.*

"I promise you, it will be okay. I will take care of you. Don't go south, go north with Susan."

I stewed. Ten minutes left. I became agitated. I tossed and turned. Could I get the money back? It was a sacrifice to pay for this trip to begin with—how could I just not show up? "This is crazy," I said to the thought in my head.

"Rob, don't go south, go north with Susan and your kids. It is okay. It is okay. I will take care of things."

I knew I had to give up the trip and go with Susan. I accepted that reality. And it felt good. I simply said, "Okay." I had made the right choice.

When the final seconds of those thirty minutes ticked away, I gently placed my hand on Susan's back. "Susan, it's time to get up."

"Huh? Oh, okay." She turned toward me, struggling to wake up. As her eyes peeked through her eyelids, she said, "Wait." And then with eyes fully open, "What are you doing in bed? What time is it?"

"It's okay. I've decided not to go to the retreat. I'm going to go with you and the kids."

"What? What are you talking about?" She was thoroughly confused.

"Yes, I've decided to spend the next few days with you and the kids. I'm going to pass on the retreat."

"But wait. This is a great opportunity for you. This doesn't make sense. Why are you doing this?" She sat up in bed and, talking very directly to me, continued to insist that I go.

"Listen, I know this is going to sound crazy, but I think God told me to go with you."

"What?" She looked at me the way I would expect anyone to look at me if I were to tell them what I just said.

"Yes, I was sitting in bed when my alarm went off, and he told me not to go to the retreat."

"What?" She was incredulous. "That doesn't make any sense. What exactly did 'God' say to you?" When she said *God*, she used her fingers as quotation marks. She wasn't mocking me or teasing me, but challenged me, for she felt the same skepticism I felt at first.

"Well, his exact words were, 'Rob, don't go south, go north with Susan.' He said that to me several times. It was the oddest thing. It came out of nowhere."

"I don't get it. That doesn't make any sense." She looked like she was deciding a dispute in her head. "No, you're going south, and I'm going north. That was the plan. We're sticking to it." She wasn't convinced this was a message from God.

"I don't think so, Susan. I spent thirty minutes arguing with the thoughts in my head about this, and I've come to realize that this is, indeed, something I need to do." I couldn't believe these words were coming out of my mouth, especially the next ones. "I want to go north with you and the kids."

"Why does he want you going north and not south? Did he tell you that?"

"Yes, he did."

This piqued her interest, though she was still resolute for an argument to send me south.

Very carefully and quietly I shared what God had shared with me: "He said, 'Susan is tethered to you, but not nearly as closely as you think.'"

Her eyes filled with tears. One streamed down her face after the other. She tried to stop them but couldn't. "No, no, I'm fine. You need to go to the retreat, I need to go north. I'll be fine," she said as she stood, attempting to hide her emotions.

I knew she would be fine, but I wasn't going south. My mind was made up. I felt God was pretty clear about it. I hugged her and held her as she eventually grew at peace with the decision too.

An hour later, I was sitting in the driver's seat of our family van. The kids were buckled in; Susan was next to me. At a stoplight, I stared at the signs in front of me. One indicated that a left turn would take me south down the interstate. The other pointed right for north. As I gently put on my right turn signal, I asked God one more time if this was the right direction. He was as clear as a bell one more time: "Rob, don't go south, go north."

I drove off, still trying to wrap my mind around the fact that I was doing this. I knew I was glimpsing what it means to walk in harmony with God, experiencing peace in decisions that are not my first choice. God has reasons, and they involve me (and you). Yes, I missed the retreat, but I gained time with my kids and more importantly, with Susan. I never believe God does anything for just one reason. Surely a multitude of things unfolded because of my decision to follow God. I may never know about them. Some would call it obedience. I say it is the adventure of a lifetime. I know the former is true, but I'm motivated by the latter.

Over the years, my friendship has blossomed with that same author. I would never have guessed it, but my trust in God's voice back then has also revealed that God is faithful throughout.

WDGWYTDWHRNITS

"Rob, do you have these experiences all the time? Is your head always hearing another voice?" I'm asked. "And if so, hearing voices in your head is something you might want to seek help for, right? You're crazy!"

The answers to these questions are no and yes. Walking in harmony with God, as I mentioned earlier, needn't be a dramatic, sensationalistic, emotional-high type of experience. Instead, it is about accepting that God is walking with you through each part of your day. From the last chapter, think of Adam and God and their walk together, before the distortion of sin.

You and I consistently make decisions. We decide which cereal to eat or how hot or cold our shower will be. We decide what clothes to wear and how much toothpaste we'll use on our toothbrush. We decide what time to leave for work and which route will be best for the traffic. All day long we make choices. Some decisions are so routine that more thought is required to even acknowledge them as choices than to choose. Cheddar or Swiss? White or wheat? Diet or regular? Medium or rare? Tall or grande? Basic choices in life face us all day long. The more difficult choices involve weighing our options, sometimes consulting friends or family. Even researching on the Internet. Do I take the job or pass on it? Which school should we put our kids in? What is the best brand of toilet to put in our new bathroom?

From the trivial to the complex, decisions can have an intermingling of the presence of God. Certainly we can make all of our own decisions. But imagine that you are someone now walking in harmony with God. And when decisions arise, what if he speaks up or intervenes? How would that change your life experience? For instance, what happens if he shows up at your regular stop at Starbucks and encourages you to bring a coffee to your coworker you've been fighting with? Or encourages you to turn your car around on your drive to work because your spouse is in pain over your earlier argument? Is that kind of life possible? And if it is, is it a hindrance to our way of life, or is it an adventure to always walk within the steps of the creator of the universe?

Some people used to wear a bracelet that had WWJD inscribed on it. The acronym meant "What Would Jesus Do?" This is a terrific question to ask as you consider doing something questionable or when you think about ways to help others. But the premise inherently misses something. That question supposes you pause the difficult situation or scene you are in, remove yourself from the picture, and place Jesus in your stead. Then you hit the "play" button and watch what he would do in the same situation. From that simulated viewing, you make your choice. A helpful tool, but it misses the natural experience of having the creator of the universe lead and guide you. If I were to design a replacement bracelet that captures the heart of what I'm saying, I would have it say WDGWYTDWHRNITS? "What does God want you to do with him right now in this situation?" This harmony is the essence of relationship. If we're still thinking of God as far away and that we're on our own here on earth, we miss out on the beauty of the relationship.

I didn't want to stop my car in the rain in order to help the woman with the flat tire. *I'm sure she's called for help*, I thought. But God "nudged" me to help.

I didn't predict I would serve as a lead pastor in a church north of Boston. But my experience with God confirms that it was his leading that placed me here.

I didn't know how important that call to my mom was one afternoon, but the thought of calling her was overwhelming. And when she asked, "How did you know to call?" I knew because God had put that thought there.

I didn't know that several weeks ago, while I was speaking to my congregation, that I would be nudged toward a "so he did" opportunity. I was in the middle of my message and a vulnerable story popped into my head to share with everyone, related to the point I was making. A split-second mental wrestling match ensued, but in the end, I shared that which was put upon me to share, even though it was hard for me. However, it was the thing that connected most with those there that day.

I didn't know God would prompt Susan and me to give money to our friends for Christmas. It seemed like a strange gift—money to friends—but this time it was something we felt burdened to do. And it wasn't a small amount. But weeks later we found out just how badly they needed it.

I didn't know I was going to write that e-mail, make that call, meet with that person, or pray with someone...on many occasions. But I want to be in a "so he did" life filled with adventure.

I didn't even know I would be writing a book, but the "nudging" from God was incessant.

This is the life I signed up for and want to live. I want to experience God in every part of my life. I don't expect it to make me a religious fanatic or out-of-touch person whom everyone is awkward around.

I don't expect that because God isn't awkward.

Instead, he created this world for us to be a part of and enjoy. And more than that, he made it possible for us to connect with the people around us. He wants more than anything for you and him to be one in that together.

CHAPTER 10

THE LAST CHAPTER

What was natural became unnatural. Through time and unfamiliarity with what was natural, the unnatural became our new natural. Until someone speaks up and announces what we've grown to accept is actually unnatural, we will continue to live with God pushed to the outer corners of our lives.

There is something better. Something that doesn't push God away.

There is something that changes it all.

We can experience God as personal and close. We can walk in harmony with him. We can know that we are his treasure and that his power reaches beyond here and into the beyond. And we can embrace his desire for us not to become more religious, but to live in his kingdom today.

And it all begins with humility. All healing and restoration of relationships begin through humility, so it is through that that we approach God and tell him, "I am sorry. I'm sorry I have kept you so far away for so long. I'm sorry I haven't brought you on this walk through life with me. And I'm sorry I relegated you to the far edges of my life."

It is possible to experience the beautiful presence of God in your life, right now. God forgives and accepts us.

The one who created the universe and set us in motion also gives us unbridled freedom in our choices. He never, ever forces us to do anything. Walking with God is like stepping into the unforced rhythms of grace. And he waits for us to discover him, like a hidden peach tree in our yards. And when we make the discovery, it is a celebration!

And in that discovery of him, God openly offers us grace and forgiveness and peace. He loves us with no conditions. Have you ever experienced God's willingness to give up everything for you? Have you felt kindness in your life that you don't deserve? Have you ever had a moment when you knew, "I just brushed up against a picture of God's love for me"? We only have to reach out and discover it.

Does life without God connect all the dots for you? Or

does the load of this world and the decisions you make create problems and questions?

The eyes of the surgeon sitting across from me in the diner were filled with sincere tears about the difficulties of his divorce years ago. He was sharing deep from his heart. He's in his early sixties and so young at heart. I love this guy.

"Rob, it was when I experienced God's grace and forgiveness that I found real freedom. Without it, I could never have experienced walking so closely with God today."

Grace takes what we've done that fights our soul and removes it. Grace is full pardon we do not deserve. Forgiveness means that we no longer have to hold our prior actions and choices against ourselves. We become freed from them. During my friend's divorce a number of years prior, he had rediscovered God. The choices he had made that led to the divorce had haunted him with guilt. He felt locked in darkness. However, in the experience of God's grace and unconditional love for him he experienced the full force of forgiveness and grace.

Yesterday my eight-year-old son, Ethan, came to me with a look of sadness on his face.

"What's wrong, buddy?" I asked.

"I did something…" He didn't finish. I sensed he wanted me to pull it from him.

"What did you do, Ethan? It's okay, you can share it."

"I set my water glass on the table, but it was too close to the edge and it fell off," he said sheepishly.

I could go a few directions in a situation like this: tell him he should look more closely before setting his drink down; yell at him for being irresponsible; discipline him so that he never again sets things down flippantly.

You might think that's overboard because it's just a broken glass, and you'd be right. But replay the scenario with Ethan dropping the glass; however, this time he decides to leave it as a mess on the floor, never telling anyone. Or say he told me about the dropped glass but then wanted me to know it wasn't really his problem because everyone drops something in their lifetime. When I receive either of those two attitudes—drop and disregard or drop and blame—discipline is called for.

Ethan did neither. He came to find me and then contritely shared the news of the dropped glass. I responded, "Ethan, it's okay. No problem. I forgive you."

It was the humility he displayed that triggered my grace and forgiveness. God is the same way. A contrite and humble heart toward God is the pathway to grace and forgiveness.

In my first few years of ministry, a couple recognized that Susan and I could use some time away. We didn't have children yet, but they saw that our work with teenagers, in my role as a youth pastor, was exhausting. "We have a home near the ocean that you are welcome to use for a week." Wow! We were touched and accepted the invitation.

Susan and I didn't know what to expect when the ferry took us two hours away to an island off the coast of Massachusetts. We were awestruck by the small town and beautiful homes. Never had we experienced anything quite like the allure of Nantucket Island.

Over the years, that couple would quietly reach out to Susan and me, even after we had children, and, as a surprise, offer us a stay at their Nantucket home. We never passed up a chance to experience that heaven on earth.

Eventually the time came for us to say good-bye to my first church. It was where I had served for thirteen years and where all our children were born. Our friendships were deep, and we felt Walnut Hill Community Church was home. So when the "nudge" or "call" came that I should lead my own church, I had mixed emotions. I was scared, but ready. We knew it was time, but were sad to leave so many who we considered family and to say good-bye to vacations on Nantucket.

About a year after we left and moved our family north of Boston where I now serve as lead pastor, I received an invitation to speak at my now-former church. The five services and the many familiar faces made it a special and emotional visit for me. After one of the services, waiting in line to meet with me, was the Nantucket couple. We hugged as they asked how we were all doing. I shared with them that leading a church was a great calling, but harder than I had anticipated. Overseeing all aspects of the church and its staff required me to develop new skills. I admitted it was difficult. And then, without forethought, I boldly asked if it would be okay if Susan and I took the kids for one more visit to their Nantucket home. They said they would be delighted to allow us a visit. We would work out the details later.

When the week finally arrived that our family was to depart for the island, we were all so excited, especially Susan and me. This visit would most likely be our last and we knew it, so we wanted to drink in the entire experience—the smell of the ferry, the smell of the Atlantic Ocean water, the view of the island town as the ferry docked in the harbor.

It was as fantastic as it had always been. That week we did all our favorite things, but most of all, we sat on the beach for hours. The days rolled by, however, and too quickly we were at the end of the week. We packed our bags, and as Susan cleaned up the home, I took the car the owners had allowed us to use all week for a car wash and gas-fill. I drove down the sandy, winding island road. I had gone about a quarter of a mile when I thought I had forgotten my wallet. I felt my pockets, turned my head downward, and looked for it on the seat next to me. "Ahhhh, there you are," I said as I grabbed it.

At that moment, I heard a loud HONK. A large truck was coming right for me because I had veered too far left on the gradual, right-bending corner. I jerked the wheel hard, sending my friend's car into a small tailspin. I averted the bulk of the oncoming truck, but our tail ends glanced each other just enough that I could feel and hear it. I slammed on the brakes and jumped out of the car. My heart was pounding. My adrenaline was pumping. But nothing compared to the rage of the woman I faced. She screamed at me, and I felt like a child in an old schoolhouse with my hand extended, waiting for the ruler to smack. It was awful. And worse, I deserved it. She said I didn't know how to drive on these sandy roads and called me a "tourist" the way one would shout a curse word.

The woman cooled just enough to inspect her vehicle and noticed that, because it was a large, weathered truck, it hadn't received any noticeable damage. She screamed once more about my "touristy incompetence" and then hopped in her cab and drove off.

Our friend's car, however, wasn't so lucky. I had damaged their property—shattered a taillight and scraped the paint. The harm was minimal, but evident. And I was sick about it. As I drove to town to gas up and wash the car, I didn't know what to do. We had tickets on a ferry for that afternoon—not enough time to get it fixed. I couldn't say nothing; that would be lying. In the end, the only thing I could do was face my friends honestly.

I left the car wash and drove back to their home and confessed about the accident to Susan. She was also distraught. Our family's goal is to always leave things that we use or borrow in as good or better condition than we received it. She knew this was the wrong way to leave the car and felt awful about how this might affect our relationship with our friends.

Time was short. I called the cab company to take us to the ferry. The kids were horsing around, and I was unusually short with them. The cab took a little longer than normal to get to the harbor, and I was frustrated by that. It was hot while we stood outside waiting for the ferry to open its doors, and I heaved mental curses toward the sun. I did all these things because I was so riddled with guilt. I knew I had to call our friends once we were settled on the two-hour crossing to the mainland, and the dread was killing me. Would they be angry? Disappointed? Would they cut off the relationship? I hated the idea of bringing this bad news. I had always treated their belongings with the highest standards. The strain of waiting grew heavier and heavier.

As the ship began its journey, I stood with the kids and Susan at the rail and watched as we pulled out of the harbor. It was a beautiful sight. But it was tainted by the inevitable and ominous call I knew I would be making in a few minutes.

We found our seats, and I headed to the snack shack to get the kids some goodies to tide them over. When I returned with the food, I told Susan, "This is it—I am going to find a remote corner on the boat and make the dreaded call."

"No problem, I'll watch the kids," she said.

It didn't take long to find a private row of interior seats as most people were outside on the deck enjoying the perfect sunny day. I sat down, turned on my phone, and found no signal. None. We were too far offshore and now on the ocean. I was helpless. I quickly surmised that I had to wait two more hours until we were near land again.

That wait proved to be agonizing. I tried to read, but soon realized I was reading the same paragraph over and over and over. I played cards with Susan, but she constantly had to poke me to remind me it was my turn. I walked the decks with my kids, but that didn't cause me to forget. The wait felt like forever.

Finally, I heard Emma yell out that she saw land. A tremendous pang of nervousness hit my heart.

I found that same quiet area, sat down, and waited for the bars on my phone to appear. Susan sat at a distance with the kids. I could see her and my children watching, knowing that something serious was going on. All of them stared at Dad, hunched, with a phone in his ear.

"Hello."

"Esther? This is Rob Strong."

"Oh, hi! How are you? I can tell that you're on the ferry by the noise and the crackling reception."

"Yes. We're just coming into port in Hyannis, but I wanted to tell you how thankful we were for our stay at your home, and—"

She cut me off. "Oh, that's great to hear. We're so happy to have you use our home. Was it a good week?"

"Well, yes. It was a tremendous week. We had a wonderful time. But I did have one problem I wanted to share with you."

Hearing my serious tone, she said, "Oh...uh...you know, Rob, Jack is right here, can you talk with him?"

Oh no. Jack. The self-made, super-successful international business owner whom my entire former church respected. And he was tough. I mean, he found Jesus in an African river after his canoe had capsized in crocodile-infested waters. He had also led the elder board for years and could alter a group discussion by simply uttering a few words. He was a man who stood out among men. And now I had to tell him I had crashed and damaged his car. I took a deep breath and held it for a moment.

"Hello?" came the deep, deep voice of Jack.

"Jack, hello, this is Rob calling from the ferry coming into Hyannis. I wanted to thank you for a very nice time at your home. But while we were there, something happened." I didn't want to beat around the bush, so I just kept talking. "In fact, it just happened a few hours ago."

"Go on."

"Well, I was driving your car into town to get gas and a car wash, and on the sandy gravel road in front of your home, I had a scary moment on the corner where a truck and your car bumped our ends together. I feel just terrible. The other car is fine, but yours—"

"Rob," he said over my words.

I didn't want to stop. I just kept speaking. "—yours has a cracked taillight and—" I had to share the guilt I felt.

"Rob."

"Yes?" I stopped rambling. My nerves were frazzled.

"Rob, I don't care about the car. Did your family have a good time, and did you get some rest?"

I couldn't speak. What was he asking me? Did he hear what I had just told him? I had harmed his personal property and treated it poorly. I wanted him to know how bad I felt. I was confused.

"Rob, are you there? Did you have a good time?"

Time was frozen. I could hear his voice, but it was almost an echo in the distance. Instead my mind was asking questions and trying to figure this all out. What was this feeling that I was experiencing? I was trying to identify it. It was unique but not unfamiliar. It was powerful and penetrated deep into my heart. What was it? I searched my mind for what felt like forever. And then I realized what it was. I was experiencing grace. When I received Jack's grace, I felt it physically lift the burden of guilt off my back, mind, and shoulders. And tears suddenly filled my eyes.

"Rob, it's okay." Upon realizing it was grace that was pouring over me, I snapped back to my senses and could hear Jack clearly. "Don't worry about the car. Cars can be fixed. We wanted your family to rest. Were you able to experience that?" His voice was still deep. It resonated into my soul. This grace from Jack was an expression of the image of God given to me.

"Yes, Jack." I struggled to talk. "Yes, we did have a wonderful time. I can't tell you how amazing it was. Thank you. But I want to pay for the damage done to your car."

"No. Don't worry about it. No problem. You go be with your family and enjoy your day. Good-bye."

"Good-bye and thank you, Jack. To both you and Esther, thank you."

I hung up the phone, dropped my head, and tried to take it all in. I was emotional and felt great at the same time. Not because I was relieved about the cost of a car repair. Not because it didn't ruin my friendship with Jack and Esther. I wept openly because I had experienced grace, firsthand. I received forgiveness that was not deserved. The weight of the situation was lifted from my back. The feeling of freedom was so tactile and present that it shook me to my bones. I wept. How could I not?

Susan and the children came and sat next to me, and she gently laid her hand on my back.

Emma, noticing my tears, spoke up first: "Daddy, what's wrong? Why are you crying?"

"Because, Emma," I said, pausing to wipe my eyes and then to look at her and the others, "because I just experienced the true feeling of grace."

When the surgeon spoke to me with the tears in his eyes and told me that it was "God's grace and forgiveness" that created freedom in his life, I remembered the taste of grace that I experienced on a ferryboat a few years earlier. My friend was right. It is only the lifting of guilt and shame that can completely free one entirely. And freedom is knowing that Jesus, who is the great lifter of guilt and shame in our spiritual and personal lives, values you as a treasure. So much so that he was willing to give up everything for you. Even his life.

Experiencing God begins with grace and forgiveness. God is pushed to the edge of your life or relegated to a role as the "Big Guy Upstairs" because of your guilt or avoidance. But he doesn't want you to feel he must be kept far away. He wants you to reach out and grab hold of him.

He wants to walk life with you. He wants you to know that you are his image in this world and that by walking with him, you can and will experience the life intended for you. You can experience life with him. God is right there with you.

My oldest son pulled me aside recently. "Dad, can we talk? Privately?" He was noticeably uncomfortable.

"Sure." We found a quiet place away from his siblings.

"Dad, I know you're writing a book about God and how people can connect with him."

"Yep." I nodded. "I am." I wasn't sure where this was going.

"Well, remember when we moved to this new state and how much it left me struggling without friends?"

Indeed, I did remember. Uprooting my family from our home in Connecticut outside of New York City after thirteen years was a very difficult time for all of us. As I mentioned earlier, all of our children were born there, and we had developed tremendous relationships. But of the six of us, it was most difficult for him specifically because he struggles with change. In fact, he will tell you he doesn't like it at all. So when we moved, he felt isolated and lonely, struggling to find an identity and to make friends.

"I remember that, very much so. It was a difficult time."

He paused for a moment to collect his thoughts and emotions. Then he continued, "When I would go to bed at night after we moved, I remembered a verse in the Bible that told me that if I cry out to God, he would listen. So I would do that. I would cry to him. I was so lonely." He looked down and put his hands to his eyes. "And I remembered that you told me that God wants to walk with me through this, that I wasn't alone, that I can talk with him. I wanted to try it. So I used to lay there in the darkness and ask God to help me through the loneliness."

To see my son in pain, but also interacting with God in a humble and intimate way was moving. It was hard to hear about his struggles, and I didn't know why he was convinced he had to tell me this story.

"Dad, God helped me through that. I felt like he was right there with me. When I didn't have friends, I just told him about it, and he was right there. And now today I have found friends I really trust."

I was encouraged by what he was sharing, but still didn't know why he wanted to share this with me.

And then he said this: "And then something happened."

The suspense was palpable, although I don't think he meant to create it. Through the fighting of his emotions, it was hard for him to get his words out.

"What happened?" I asked.

"Well, while I was thinking about it all and what happened, I felt like . . ." Tears welled up in his eyes. "I felt like God was nudging me to tell you to add my story to your book. For days it seemed like he kept telling me to tell you." ·

And ... so he did.

He continued, "I felt like God nudged me, and that if it can help someone else know about walking with God, then I want you to share it."

And ... so I did.

ACKNOWLEDGMENTS

Craig and Amy Mowrey, Ed and Niro Feliciano, Brad and Leslie Creel, Scott and Jennifer Rupff, Ray and Nancy Mowrey...you all were there during a very transformational time in my life. I love you guys.

Joel and Sharon Eidsness, Clive and Ruth Calver...you guided me to this point as my mentors and friends. Thank you for your investment in me.

In the early 2000s I found myself immersed in Core and its Creative Team. Thank you...you know who you are. Some of what was written in this book came from our times of study together. A.J. and Mirjam Picard, Adam and Carrie DePasquale...a special thank-you.

Todd and Tami Ingersoll...if there were ever people in my life who I knew would be there for me/us no matter what, it is you two. Thank you.

Rob and Kristen Bell...you have been our friends for a long, long time. Kindred spirits. You are treasures to Susan and me.

Jason (Jay) Ford. Love you, man. You, too, John Gaynor.
Tim Popadic, thank you for being a great friend.

Jed Mullenix, you are a brother in this crazy business.

The Great Brione, you were there from the beginning.

Chris Ferebee and Wendy Grisham...you believed in me. Thank you.

My staff...Matt Beattie, Jake Scott, Mike Adams, Priscilla Sellers, Patti Quigley, Kristine Rego, Tobias Marx, Dave Astolfi, Mary Allen, Joyce Goldthwaite. And my board members...Bill Keating, Jim Andreson, Fred Budd, Jeff Palmer, Chip Spengler, Tim Slighter, Ben Nyce. You threw your support around me and I appreciate that. And my like-brothers and sisters...Randy and Kim Young, Kenny and Shayne Mitchell, Bernie and Blaire Prusaczyk, Dave and Maddie Gallo, Ben and Laurie Rockney. The Kitchen Adventures crew. And the church I call family—Grace Community. I wish I could keep naming the many, many people who deserve it.

Ralph and Carolyn Guiduli, it is great being a part of your family.

Mom and Dad...thank you for everything. I love you.

Parker, Emma, Ethan, and Addison. Yes, you four are pretty awesome.

Most of all, I want to thank Susan. I love you. And I have one question for you: "BWMF?"

ABOUT THE AUTHOR

Rob Strong is currently serving as the lead pastor of Grace Community, a church located just north of Boston, MA. His nearly twenty years of ministry have been intentionally located in the states called New England, where he loves the people and also where he believes the future of Christianity will be born. Rob has a wife and four children. Follow Rob on Twitter @therobstrong, and read more or schedule a speaking engagement on his websites: thebigguyupstairs.com and therobstrong.com.